ANGER
RAGE
DANGER

ANGER
RAGE
DANGER

With God's help I was
transformed into a
peaceful person

Faith A. Madison

XULON ELITE

Xulon Press Elite
555 Winderley Pl, Suite 225
Maitland, FL 32751
407.339.4217
www.xulonpress.com

Exulon Elite

© 2024 by Faith A. Madison

All rights reserved solely by the author. The author guarantees all contents are original and do not infringe upon the legal rights of any other person or work. No part of this book may be reproduced in any form without the permission of the author.

Due to the changing nature of the Internet, if there are any web addresses, links, or URLs included in this manuscript, these may have been altered and may no longer be accessible. The views and opinions shared in this book belong solely to the author and do not necessarily reflect those of the publisher. The publisher therefore disclaims responsibility for the views or opinions expressed within the work.

Unless otherwise indicated, Scripture quotations taken from the King James Version (KJV) – *public domain.*

Scripture quotations taken from the Holy Bible, New International Version (NIV). Copyright © 1973, 1978, 1984, 2011 by Biblica, Inc.™. Used by permission. All rights reserved.

Scripture quotations taken from the Holy Bible, New Living Translation (NLT). Copyright ©1996, 2004, 2007 by Tyndale House Foundation. Used

Scripture quotations taken from New Life Version (NLV). Copyright © 1969 by Christian Literature International. by permission of Tyndale House Publishers, Inc.

Scripture quotations taken from the New King James Version (NKJV). Copyright © 1982 by Thomas Nelson, Inc. Used by permission. All rights reserved.

Scripture quotations taken from the New American Standard Bible (NASB). Copyright © 1960, 1962, 1963, 1968, 1971, 1972, 1973, 1975, 1977, 1995 by The Lockman Foundation. Used by permission. All rights reserved.

Scripture quotations taken from the Good News Bible © 1994 published by the Bible Societies/HarperCollins Publishers Ltd UK, Good News Bible© American Bible Society 1966, 1971, 1976, 1992. Used with permission.

Paperback ISBN-13: 978-1-66289-449-7
Hardcover ISBN-13: 978-1-66289-656-9
eBook ISBN-13: 978-1-66289-450-3

And we know that all things work together for good to those who love God, to those who are the called according to His purpose.
Romans 8:28 (NKJV)

I can do all things through Christ who strengthens me.
Philippians 4:13 (NKJV)

TABLE OF CONTENTS

Introduction xiii
1   My Childhood through College Years 1
2   My Life in Four Different States 15
3   Admitting I had a Problem 19
4   The Healing Process 21
5   What is Love? 25
6   Satan's Way to Trigger my Anger 28
7   Do You Wear a Mask? 31
8   The People of Hanfield and Baby Steps 33
9   Visionaries ABF and Telling of My Anger 36
10   Forgiveness, Grace, and Mercy 44
11   Running and Endurance 53
12   My Baptism 57
13   Bullied and Molested 67
14   The Big Picture and God's Plan 71
15   The Recording in My Head 81
16   God's Love, Anger, and Punishment 84
17   Give it to God 87
18   Reminders from God 92

19	Are you a Prodigal Son or Daughter?	96
20	We all Can Change	100
21	Lofty Goals and Perfectionism	106
22	Anger and Rage Resurfacing	110
23	There is Hope - You are a Work in Progress	113

Endnotes 127

INTRODUCTION

Danger.... Have you ever heard the saying "anger is only one letter away from danger"? Well, it is. Add the letter "D" to the front and you now have Danger. I had heard that saying before, but I never realized this next thing until I started writing this book. Have you ever noticed there is also another perilous word within the word danger? Drop the "D" and you're back to anger. Now if you drop the "N" and move the "R" to the front, you now have rage. I have experienced all three of these words. Anger can, and will often, lead to rage. Rage can then lead to a multitude of dangerous things, one example many of us can relate to is road rage. How many times have you seen something on TV or online that has to do with road rage? I've been there and done that. I'm not proud of it, but rage is now a part of my history. At least my rage didn't culminate in a serious or fatal accident. It could have, but luckily it didn't. Actually it wasn't luck. It was God.

I looked up the definitions for both anger and rage in the *Merriam Webster Dictionary*. I found the following:

Anger:

"a strong feeling of displeasure and usually of antagonism"

Rage:

"violent and uncontrolled anger"

"a fit of violent wrath"

"violent action" (as of wind or sea)

"an intense feeling"

    I find it interesting that there was only one definition of anger, but more than one definition for rage. The one referenced that says a violent action (as of wind or sea), in my experience, it can be any violent action, as you will see in my story.
    Anger is an emotion given to us by God to express a wrong that someone has committed against us. God did not intend for us to turn this worthwhile emotion into an action of rage, which can hurt others as well as ourselves. This is when anger becomes sin. For example, when someone says or does something to us that angers us, we scream at that person or even worse, resort to violence. Another one is road rage. Someone cuts us off on the road, which makes

us angry, and we try to chase that person down and do the same thing. Both are examples of when anger becomes sin.

If someone had told me when I was in my twenties (about forty years ago) how God was going to work in my life, I would have told them they were crazy. At the time I'd never believe I'd live in Indiana; admit I had an anger problem, needed counselling; enjoy Christian music; attend church on a regular basis; become a Christian; get baptized; and write a book about my testimony.

Many years ago, the radio station I listen to, WBCL, a Christian station based in Ft. Wayne, IN, had a question for the listening audience. The question was, "If you were able to go back and change something in your past, what would it be?" I e-mailed my response that said I would change most of my life. I also gave them a small amount of my story. This is what my story is all about and how God has used it all for my good, and possibly for your good. You just need to ask.

MY CHILDHOOD THROUGH COLLEGE YEARS

I grew up in a suburb of Boston, MA called Reading back in the sixties and seventies. I did not get much positive feedback from my mother. But dad was always positive. I remember him saying "whatever you do, give it your best." I don't ever recall seeing him negative. Mom was a stay-at-home mom and dad worked. So, when things happened, she was the first one I'd go to when there was a problem. When I was bullied by kids at school and the neighborhood boys on the way home, I would be crying when I got home and told my mom what happened. She would tell me not to cry because they would know they got the better of me. Then in almost the same breath, she'd ask me what I did to provoke it, as if it was my fault. This went on all through elementary school. During the Summer I went to Girl Scout Camp. A bus would bring me back from camp and the drop off point was near the elementary school I attended. There usually was one of the boys, I'll call "Mike" waiting there to pick on me. I was always so scared and looking out the window of the bus to see if anyone was there. If I did see "Mike", I would beg the bus driver to drop me off further down the street, but that never happened. One time, "Mike" chased me up the hill to the school. I was so scared and cried because I did not know what he would do to me. I ran up the stairs, screamed for help and pounded on the door trying to get someone's attention as he punched me in the back. No one was there. "Mike" finally left and I went home crying. I got no sympathy from my mom.

According to my parents, prior to the third grade I was creative and the typical kid who would hide under the covers with a book and a flashlight. What's interesting is that I do not remember this at all. All I do remember is that I didn't (and still don't) really like to read. As it turns out, my third-grade teacher took all of this away from me. She thought there was something wrong with me. At the time I was frequently being taken to a different area of the school to take many tests. I assume the tests I was given were to find out what was wrong with me, if anything. With all this going on, somehow the reading and the creativity all disappeared. The only information the test administrator could tell my parents was that there was nothing wrong with me, but that I was more left-handed than most right-handed people are. What I mean by this is I can do a few things with my left hand. I am not ambidextrous. I brush my teeth and through a frisbee with my left hand and can not do these with my right hand. I attribute this to my being taught these things by one of my parents. If a person is right or left-handed, normally they can not use their other hand to do things. I'm the only right-handed person in my immediate family. Both my parents and my sister are left-handed. Years later, my parents told me that after this all happened, they had met with the principal to decide who my teachers would be for the fourth through sixth grades.

This is probably about the time when I started to withdraw. If I would answer a question the teacher asked and got it wrong, everyone would laugh at me. By the end of the fourth grade, I was failing in reading. My parents gave me the choice to either attend summer school or stay back a year. I chose summer school. I still didn't like to read. If anything, it made me like it even less because I was being forced to read. I didn't like my fifth grade teacher very much. But I didn't understand back then that he was trying to help me. When I would do a good job on a paper, he would always write on it "great job I have faith in you." I was always so embarrassed. To me, he was picking on me. But many years later, I realized that he was trying to pick me up and make me realize I was doing good work. He was and is very devout in his faith and a great person. Something I didn't know about him until I graduated from high school was that he saved papers from every student he taught and sent them back to them at graduation.

He sent me two poems I had written. At the bottom of both was that phrase, "I have faith in you."

I am the older of two daughters. Unfortunately, I admit I was a horrible older sister. I used to bully my sister, Patti. I would tease her and even hit her. I would do these things until she was about to cry and then I'd do everything I could to get her not to so I wouldn't get into trouble. Sometimes it worked, but when it didn't work, I did get into trouble.

At the age of about 11 or 12, I started babysitting for a couple families that had moved into the neighborhood. One family, I would take care of two girls on Saturdays so the mom could run errands since the father I'll call "Robert" worked. I was molested and raped by this man and this went on for about a year. At that time, earning my own money was important to me. It meant that I would be able to buy things that I wanted or put the money in the bank. Every time I was to babysit on a Saturday for them, I remember I would pray that "Robert" would not come home at lunchtime. And every Saturday, he would come home for lunch. At the time I didn't know why I couldn't tell anyone or get help. But after years of counseling, I realized it was because my mom had led me to believe from an early age that everything that happened to me was my fault.

My Father passed away in 2003 never knowing about my having been molested by the neighbor. My mother is now in memory care, and I have never told her. However, I had told my sister years later while I was in counselling.

You may be asking where God was during my year of sexual assault. He was right there with me. I didn't get pregnant, contract any diseases, or physically injured. He knew how things would turn out. God did not cause this to happen to me, Satan did. But God knew where it would lead me. So often, people blame God for the adverse things that happen to them. God does not cause bad things to happen, Satan causes the adversity. ***The thief does not come except to steal, and to kill and to destroy. I have come that they may have life, and that they may have it more abundantly. (John 10:10) NKJV*** But God may allow adverse things to happen because He sees the big picture and knows where we will end up. He also knows we will be stronger on the other side of it.

ANGER RAGE DANGER

Mom and Dad in Happier Times

Patti & me with our dog Duchess

MY CHILDHOOD THROUGH COLLEGE YEARS

Mom, Dad, Patti & me with Duchess on Vacation

High School Picture

Graduation Day - Mom, Dad Patti & me

Graduation Day - Grandma & me

As I was growing up, we went to church every week. There was Sunday School for the elementary school kids. What is so strange is that out of all those years I can only remember one Sunday School class. It was when I was chosen to collect the offering for the class. As I was taking the basket to the front of the class, I slipped on the hardwood floor, fell and dropped the basket of money, and everyone started to laugh at me. When I was in high school, I went to Church in the mornings and attended youth group at night. I never really understood what was being said during the church service or how scripture related to everyday life. I also don't remember anything being said about being born again in Christ or accepting Christ into my heart. I do remember that when I used to sit in church, I would count the number of times the minister said the word faith. Every time the word faith was said, it dug at me. I don't know if it was my pride or the fact that I had little faith in God and His plan for my life.

In elementary school, there was one boy that was actually a friend. I'll call him "Peter." He was a friend from first grade through maybe the fifth or sixth grade. What I remember about "Peter" is that he was good at art. At least I thought he was. But this was also first and second grade art. He used to draw animals, cut them out and give them to me. But he was also nice to me and didn't pick on me. In the later years, he would sit with me at lunch, and made me laugh. I also used to go to his house to visit. He was just a friend that I liked because he didn't pick on me. By the time I was entering into junior high school, I had no interest in boys. I wasn't being bullied anymore but had no interest. This is because most of the guys that bullied me went to a different junior high school than I did. However, "Peter's" family had moved away. This meant I no longer had a friend that was a guy.

My lack of faith in God's love and plan had me looking for love from men and relationships. During the summer between my freshman and sophomore years of high school, a friend of mine, I'll call "Martha" introduced me to someone, I'll call "Carl." In the fall of that same year, "Carl" asked me out on a date. While we were dating, I remember I couldn't wait to talk to him on the phone or to see him. I thought I was "in love" with him almost from day one. We were together for a very long time. Even after he graduated high school and joined the military, we continued the relationship. The following year, I graduated high school and went off to college and we continued in a relationship. Things were great between us during those years.

About a month into my freshman year of college I was out walking around campus, and I met a guy I'll call "Max" who asked me if I wanted to go to the bar. At that time, the drinking age was eighteen. It would have been about another month before I turned eighteen, but since I didn't know anyone and someone asked me to do something, I went along with it. Unfortunately, one of my drinks had been drugged. I ended up in his room. To this day, I still do not know how I got to his room or if anything happened. That was the start of my promiscuity, drinking and smoking pot. After this incident, I went to counseling at college for a very short time. For some reason, I wanted to see "Max" again. At least I didn't remember what dorm he was in and didn't see him around campus. All of this even though I had a boyfriend who

I loved very much. I transferred schools my sophomore year and met up with someone I knew of in high school. We became "friends." He was someone I became more promiscuous with. We also smoked pot and drank. Again, God was with me through all of it. I never got pregnant, contracted any diseases, or became addicted to drugs.

The summer between my sophomore and junior years of college, I found out my dad would be leaving us. He said my parent's marriage had been going downhill since the early to mid 1960s. He finally had had enough. He told me that the only reason he stuck it out for as long as he did was because of my sister and me. I had no idea there was a problem in the marriage. At the time, I thought their breakup did not bother me. I wanted them to be happy. By the end of the first semester of my junior year, I was on academic probation. By the middle of my second semester, I was flunking out. So, I decided to drop out a couple months before the school year finished. Hopefully doing this would save what credits I had. It took another few years before I finally admitted that my parent's separation had greatly impacted me.

I had not even told my parents I was dropping out of school. By this time, my boyfriend, "Carl" was stationed in New England. He came to school, picked me up and we headed to his apartment. My parents found out and they were not happy. They made me go home which meant that I was going to have to move back to my mom's house.

After that, I got a job in Boston at an insurance company, which I enjoyed very much. Almost every Friday, I would leave work, head for the bus station and go to be with "Carl" for the weekend. Most weekends he had to work the overnight shift. So, if he had to work, I went on base with him, and we'd talk while he worked. Periodically I would bring stuff from work to keep me busy. Going to visit him served two purposes. I loved him and wanted to be with him. But it also got me away from home. Mom and I never had a close relationship anyway and it got even worse after my parents split up. She tried to brainwash me against my dad. I was not going to let that happen. Staying neutral proved to be very difficult. Unfortunately, when I went to visit "Carl", there were many times we would have some bad arguments. When I look back, I was the one that started them, and they were always over stupid stuff. Most of the time I would just pick and pick until it erupted. It never got physical. Just a lot of yelling. I was trying to control everything, including him. Even though he loved me, the arguing didn't seem to bother him. It probably did, he just didn't let on. He did ask me to marry him a few years later. Unfortunately, a year or so after we were engaged, I broke it off. The reason I gave was that we fought too much, and I could not see us going into a marriage that way. What I didn't know at that time was I had anger issues. If we had married, I don't think it would have lasted because I didn't know I had a problem. I would not have been a good wife and mother, but God knew.

MY LIFE IN FOUR DIFFERENT STATES

Somewhere around 1980-1981, I had moved in with a married couple. I had known the wife for many years from church. After about a year of seeing her on the train, she asked me to move in with them. It would help them out with rent and allow me to move out of my mom's house. My relationship with my mom had gotten worse, so it sounded like a good idea at the time. I decided to move in with them. Unbeknownst to me at the time she had planned this all out. After I had been living with them for a while, she left her husband.

In 1982, Mom remarried and moved to Maine and Patti went with her. I also moved to Florida with a man I'll call "George." I had no idea what I was getting myself into. I didn't have a relationship with him until a year or so later. But it was not a good one. Once in Florida, I had job issues and my anger started to grow. Two different times, I got physical and hit him as I was screaming at him. I was so angry and hit him so hard that the blood vessels in one of my hands and wrist had burst. The second time this happened, it really scared me, and I swore I would never hit someone again. I still didn't know I had an anger problem. I just had a temper, and believed it was his fault. In 1986, the relationship ended, and I moved back to Massachusetts and lived in Woburn, a town near Reading.

Patti & me at Mom's house. Having Fun

With our old Scout Uniforms

Once back in Massachusetts, I looked up a few of my old friends from high school and got a new job in Boston. Several years after I moved back to Massachusetts, "George" came to live with me and we got back together. After a couple more years, he decided to move to Indiana and then a year or so after that I moved there to be with him. However, there was a person who I'll call "Jack" that I had grown close to and had feelings for. Since I felt my feelings were being not being reciprocated, I decided to move to Indiana to be with "George". At the time, I felt that I would be with someone who wanted to have a relationship with me. A day or so before I left Massachusetts, myself, "Jack" and another friend, I'll call "Elaine" went out for a drink. "Jack" asked me if I loved him, referring to "George." I remember hesitating and then saying "yes." When I think back about that incident, my hesitation should have told me that I really didn't love "George" like I thought I did. It didn't take too long before I realized that "George" didn't want a relationship, he wanted a housekeeper.

I found out after living in Indiana for several years that "Jack" did have feelings for me and that I had broken his heart when I left.

In 1994, I was living in another new state. I hadn't been to church since I was in my teens. I did go to a church a few times with "George." I don't remember much about this church except that they had services Sunday mornings, Sunday and Wednesday evenings. We didn't go very often though. I began withdrawing. I had issues at my jobs again and I would start fights with him at any chance I had. I would pick and nag until we would start arguing. In 1997, he ended the relationship because he was with someone else. This was the final ending of our very long on again off again relationship. The person he was with was young enough to be my daughter. "George" is four years older than me. I found a place that I could afford and moved out.

ADMITTING I HAD A PROBLEM

At the time all this was happening, I finally realized and admitted I had an anger problem. I also realized that "George" was verbally and emotionally abusive. It was very subtle, and I don't even know if he realized he was being abusive. Or maybe he knew exactly what he was doing. I honestly think that he thought he was joking. I was now living in Indiana, which is in the "Bible belt." (The "Bible belt" is an area chiefly in the southern U.S. whose inhabitants are believed to hold uncritical allegiance to the literal accuracy of the Bible.) I found a counselor and made an appointment. A few days after I made the appointment, I called back and cancelled because I realized she was associated with a Christian organization. Since I had not been to church in several years, I was not ready to have the Bible "rammed down my throat." At least this is what I thought would happen. What was completely strange, at the time, was that a few more days passed, and I called back and set up the appointment again. God knows what we need and what God wants is always what we need. God knew that I needed to go to this counselor, Bonnie Huxford. He knew that through her working with me, she would be one of the pieces to bring me back to Him. When I got there, of course I was nervous and did not know what to expect. Bonnie made me feel very comfortable, at least as much as I could be in a "strange" situation. She had me complete a survey that would determine where I was on the anger spectrum. Not only did it indicate that I was an angry person, but that I needed to seek someone out immediately. Thus, the counseling started.

THE HEALING PROCESS

Bonnie was and still is a wonderful person. I keep in touch with her even though I'm no longer a patient. She didn't "ram the Bible down my throat" like I thought she would. We talked a lot and she started by using the science of psychology. I had to remember and relive different parts of my life. I don't remember exactly when it happened, but I finally dealt with the molestation and rape from my childhood and cried the whole time I was in our session. In a way it was traumatic reliving that part of my life and everything "Robert" did to me. When I got home that evening, I wrote "Robert" a letter which I couldn't send since I didn't know where he lived. Instead, I gave it to Bonnie the next time I saw her.

I tried to contact the State of Massachusetts to see if there was anything I could do to bring charges against him. But in the State of Massachusetts, because I never forgot the incident and then resurfacing and I was over 18 years old, there was no recourse. This was so upsetting to me since I was 11 or 12 years old at the time of the incident. I didn't have much of a choice since I was a young girl, and he was a much larger and stronger person. Since I didn't have a good relationship with my mom, I had no one to turn to and tell. I do think of "Robert" at times and wonder if he ever did this to another young girl. I hope he didn't. I called my sister, Patti and apologized to her for the way I had treated her when we were growing up. We both started crying. She told me there was nothing to apologize for, but she did forgive me. I also told her about my being molested and who did it. Needless to say, Patti was quite shocked and upset hearing this.

In the early years of my counseling, Bonnie gave me a Bible that was easy to read. She introduced me to Joyce Meyer Ministries on video and on audio tape. I finally started going back to church on a regular basis and accepted Christ into my life and heart. A year or so went by and I found Joyce Meyer on TV and started watching. When I started listening to her, I found I could relate so much to what she was talking about. She had had a rough childhood for many years and had become controlling. She also explains how scripture relates to life. I never knew scripture did relate to everyday life.

In the front of this book, I referenced the following scripture: **And, we know that all things work together for good to those who love God, to those who are the called according to His purpose. (Romans 8:28) NKJV** This is a scripture Bonnie gave to me near the beginning of my counseling. She asked me if I knew of it. I told her I didn't as I didn't really know any scriptures then. So, at that time, it was the first one I can say that I learned. This scripture is so true. It is not just the good things, but every bad thing that happens to us can and will be worked out for the good.

When I started going back to church, I was still a very angry person. I would go in, sit in the back corner close to the door, and ignore everyone around me. At a point in the service when we were asked to turn and greet each other, I would either go out the door to avoid this or I would sit with my head down reading the bulletin. If someone greeted me, I would acknowledge them by saying "hi, but not anything more. I didn't even smile or make eye contact.

At this same time, I was dating a new guy I'll call "John," who was not good for me either. He was able to manipulate people into thinking that things were great. Unfortunately, he was an alcoholic. I did not know this until after I was with him for a while. He would ask me to come by after work. Since I was thinking he was asking for us to go out on a date, I would go. However, I would often get to his house, and he would not be there. There were times that he would not show up for hours. As it turns out, he was at the bar. If he was at the house, we would go out after work, but I felt it was more for me to be his designated driver. Once we got to the bar, he would sit for a little bit with me and then leave me to go be with other people he knew. I was left to sit alone the whole time we were there. This of course made me angry. But, since I thought I "loved" him, I didn't want to say or do anything. I had someone who was somewhat paying attention to me. Then when we would finally leave, I'd be extremely ticked off and start yelling at him. These types of things didn't stop me from being with him. I kept going back when he'd call thinking he wanted to be with me. I would do all kinds of things for him; clean up his house, wash the dishes, or wash his clothes. He'd say something about going out to eat, but that always meant he wanted me to pay. So, I did every time. After the relationship was over, I realized all I was trying to do was buy the relationship by paying for everything. It didn't work. But it worked for him. He was able to get a lot of free meals and a lot of other things with my money.

    I was dating "John" during the early years of my counselling. I remember telling Bonnie about the things that were going on. She obviously knew this was not a good relationship but wanted me to figure it out for myself. One time she asked me how I would feel if the relationship with "John" were to end. However, if I remember right, I dodged the question and said that I could help him. What I learned from counselling and God's Word is that the only person who each one of us can help "fix" is ourselves. We cannot "fix" another person. Only God can do that and each of us must choose to want to be helped.

WHAT IS LOVE?

While working on this book, I remembered there was a scripture that I did know prior to the one I included in the beginning of this book. I learned it on a church youth group retreat when I was in high school. It is **1 Corinthians 13 (Good News for Modern Man, 1966)**. This chapter is known as the Love Scripture. This is one of the thirteen books (letters) Paul wrote. This is what he wrote to the Church in Corinth:

> *I may be able to speak the languages of men and even of angels, but if I have not love, my speech is no more than a noisy gong or a clanging bell. I may have the gift of inspired preaching; I may have all knowledge and understand all secrets; I may have all the faith needed to move mountains—but if I have not love, I am nothing. I may give away everything I have, and even give up my body to be burned—but if I have not love, it does me no good. Love is patient and kind; love is not jealous, or conceited, or proud; love is not ill-mannered, or selfish, or irritable; love does not keep a record of wrongs;*

love is not happy with evil but is happy with the truth. Love never gives up; its faith, hope, and patience never fail. Love is eternal. There are inspired messages, but they are temporary; there are gifts of speaking, but they will cease; there is knowledge, but it will pass. For our gifts of knowledge and of inspired messages are only partial; but when what is perfect comes, then what is partial will disappear. When I was a child, my speech, feelings, and thinking were all those of a child; now that I am a man, I have no more use for childish ways. What we see now is like the dim image in a mirror; then we shall see face to face. What I know now is only partial; then it will be complete, as complete as God's knowledge of me. Meanwhile these three remain: faith, hope, and love; and the greatest of these is love.

This is a beautiful scripture. Love is a verb and a noun. When I first learned about this scripture, I had no idea what love was all about. I was dating "Carl" at the time, but thought it was all about the human kind of love. It is, but it really isn't. It's so much more. It's about the love we receive from God which is unconditional love. Once we receive it, we are then able to give it to others. Since I did not know what love was back then (or most of my years), I was not able to receive it much less give it.

In verses 4 and 5 Paul says, **Love is patient and kind; it is not jealous or conceited or proud; love is not ill-mannered or selfish or irritable; love does not keep a record of wrongs.** I was not patient or kind. I was jealous, had a lot of pride, was ill-mannered, selfish, irritable and I did keep records of wrongs done to me by others. Hmmm..... guess I really didn't have the love thing going on in my life after all. I now know I didn't even love myself. So, how could I truly love others. Loving ourselves is not being "in love" with ourselves. It's, just loving the person that we are and should be. We must live with ourselves twenty-four hours a day, seven days a week, and 365 days a year. So, we need to love who we are.

There's a saying that's been around for a long time. Treat others the way you want to be treated. Another ah ha moment. I certainly didn't treat others the way I wanted to be treated, then wondered why I got treated poorly. At times I never realized why I was being mistreated or that I was being mistreated at all.

In all my years, I have dated only three guys. Unfortunately, the second and third ones were not good to me. They were emotionally abusive and took advantage of me. The flipside though is that I was not the best person either. Because I didn't know what love was, I was abusive and controlling. I'd like to think I didn't take advantage of them, but maybe I did.

SATAN'S WAY TO TRIGGER MY ANGER

A few years passed and I was still going to counseling. At one point, I had decided to quit my job and work on obtaining my CDL license. This meant I had to stop going to counseling. But I also felt I really didn't need it anymore. I "was doing well." This was Satan lying to me again. I did obtain my CDL license, was hired by a trucking company, and started to drive with a trainer. This didn't last very long. My trainer did not give positive feedback. I knew this up front. He had told me he does not give positive feedback. But I was fine. I didn't need it. As it turns out, it wasn't a good thing. I felt like I was an accident waiting to happen. You certainly can't feel that way when you're driving a semi. After one week of driving, I got off the truck and headed home. I now needed a job. I was able to find a job at a popcorn factory. It wasn't a difficult job, but it was hard on your body because you're standing twelve hours a day.

    I remember many, many years ago, there were people who had committed crimes and would blame music for their actions. They'd say, "the music made me do it." I thought this is ridiculous. Music can't make you do things. But, I found out firsthand that we can be influenced by the music we listen to. I'm not saying that the music makes us do things, but we can be influenced by it. There was, a style of music that triggered a different attitude in me. At that time, it was anger. This was rap music. It took a while for me to realize what was happening. When I worked at the popcorn factory it was being played quite a bit of the time. Even though I couldn't hear the words, I could tell it was the wrong kind of music for me. I could feel my blood pressure rising and my anger building. I realized that when I was away from it, I was calm. I'm not saying that music should be used as an excuse, but it can cause issues. I say cause issues, not make you do something wrong.

This kind of music was played periodically at the bars that "John" and I frequented. I could barely make it through one song, but if another played, I had to leave. One evening, I don't remember if this was being played or not, I was sitting at the bar, and he was off talking with other people as usual. The guy sitting next to me was a friend of "John's" and I knew him a little. He was telling me that I needed to get "John" out of there. He told me the guys "John" was talking to at the end of the bar were going to cause trouble for him. I knew that if "John" didn't want to leave, there was nothing I could do to make him. Mind you, at this point, I had not been to counselling in a long time. One of the guys at the end of the bar, sucker punched "John". He was now laid out on the floor. To this day, I do not remember getting up off the barstool and going to the end of the bar. I was standing (straddling) over "John" ready to deck the guy that did it. The only thing that was stopping me was the bartender. I was so full of rage that I didn't care what I was about to do. I was arguing with the bartender that I wanted a piece of the guy standing behind her. No one was going to hurt a person that I cared about. I don't even remember moving away and sitting back down. The guys that started the altercation were told to leave. I was almost thrown out too, but since I didn't do anything else, they let me stay. "John" ended up with a black eye and asked me to lie to his kids about what happened. I kept the lie.

This was the only time I can remember feeling the way I did. What I was feeling was the kind of rage that could have caused a lot of problems for a lot of people including myself. My blood pressure was up and I felt invincible. I wanted to take on a guy in a fight because of what he had done. There were times that I would feel a milder version of this when I'd be driving. But it never got to this extent. But rage is rage, no matter how mild or strong. Just like sin is sin. There is no little sin and no big sin. It's all sin.

DO YOU WEAR A MASK?

Being angry is very debilitating. It can cause depression, which Bonnie said I also had. When some people are hurting, they have eating disorders, cut themselves or can become depressed. Until a person deals with what happened in the past to get past the hurt done to them, they cannot go forward in a healthy way. I had no idea that I was depressed. I felt like I was a happy person. But that was just the mask I would put on for everyone else to see, including myself. But I didn't even know I was putting on a mask.

Ever since I was in high school, I've been in a customer service type job. I've worked retail and in offices. Having anger issues is not a good thing when working in positions where you deal with other people. If a customer gets upset or starts yelling, it's very hard to not get angry and raise your voice back at them. What makes things even worse is that my voice tends to carry anyway. So, if I get upset the volume of my voice tends to go up. This is not good when you work in close proximity with others.

I mentioned earlier about a mask we put on when we want others to see something different than what we are really feeling. My school and work friends from Massachusetts were completely unaware I had anger issues. When I told a few of them I had anger issues and, that I was in counseling, they were very surprised. They had no idea because I always wore the "mask." I let people see what I wanted people to see, which was that I was happy, and I was doing ok.

We all wear a mask. What does your mask look like and how long have you been wearing it? What does it say about you and what are you hiding?

THE PEOPLE OF HANFIELD AND BABY STEPS

While I was in counselling, I started going back to church on a regular basis. I was invited to go to Hanfield Methodist Church. The first time I went in and listened to the pastor and his message, I was hooked. The music was wonderful, and Pastor Tim Helm preached in a way I had not heard before. He read the scriptures, but he also explained how they relate to everyday life. I needed this as I was still a very angry person and had trouble connecting the Bible and church sermons to everyday life. If you think about it, what's interesting is how something that was written over 2000 years ago is still very valid to our lives today. If we would only read the Bible, we would find that it is a roadmap to how we need to act and how to deal with what is happening day to day.

At that time, I was still with "John". He would not attend church. But that was because he was usually nursing a hangover. I couldn't even get him to start going to a later service. When our relationship finally ended, I was driving a 1985 Ford F150 about sixty-five miles roundtrip every day to work. At that time, I sporadically attended Hanfield because of the extra gas it took to get there. Gas was almost five dollars a gallon at that time, and I had to fill the tank twice a week. Unbeknownst to me, a friend of mine, Debbie Edwards had been in contact with Hanfield and asked if they would be on the lookout for a better vehicle for me. In a matter of just a couple weeks, she was taking me to someone's house to get the car. The people at Hanfield had pooled their funds and purchased a car for me. I was so touched that people I didn't even know or talk to would come together to buy a car for me. These are the kind of people that attend Hanfield. They were (and are) very caring people. Sadly, I still didn't do much talking to people after that. If someone said "hi," I did answer them back. As the saying goes, baby steps. This is what being a Christian is all about. Helping those who are in need, whether you know them or not.

    Among the announcements every week, there was always mention of a Women's Bible Study. Unfortunately, for a long time I was unable to attend because it was offered only in the mornings, and I worked. Then an evening class was started. I didn't really want to go because I wouldn't know anyone. But, as always, God was calling me or "smacking me upside the head" and telling me I needed to do this to get to know people. I took a chance and signed up. This was something I needed. Studying God's word in addition to hearing it at the regular Sunday service. Each week in Bible Study, we were asked how we could pray for each other. I was having issues at the place I worked at but was uncomfortable about speaking up in front of others. About all I would say would be to pray about my work situation. Some people would speak up during prayer and mention a person in our group. I didn't speak up but would always pray in silence for each one. These women were great for me. We would laugh together, cry together, and support each other during times of need.

VISONAIRES ABF AND TELLING OF MY ANGER

Hanfield also offered something called ABF groups Sunday mornings. ABF stands for Adult Bible Fellowship. This is Sunday school for the adults. But I was not quite ready to start another group where I knew no one. I still wasn't comfortable around people I did not know. But of course, God "made me" seek out a class. The class I started going to is called Visionaries. I was very nervous about entering this class, but when I walked in, there were two or three women who I had already met in the Women's Bible Study. This made me feel a little more comfortable. But like the Bible Study, I didn't speak up much. This class was and is still led by a man named Gary Miller. He is very knowledgeable about the Bible and studies a lot for the lesson he will be giving the following Sunday. He planned on getting through a lesson on one Sunday, however, it usually took a couple weeks to get through it. But the lessons generate a lot of conversation in the classes which is what I think this is all about. Asking questions about what we may not understand about the Bible. I was as much at ease listening to Gary as I was with Pastor Tim and learned a lot. Gary also explained how what we were studying related to our lives.

Many years ago, Gary started teaching about the Sermon on the Mount. This is found in the **Gospel of Matthew, chapters** 5-7. These chapters talk about what we need to do to be in Christ.

> *Blessed are the poor in spirit, for theirs is the kingdom of heaven. Blessed are those who mourn, for they will be comforted. Blessed are the meek, for they will inherit the earth. Blessed are those who hunger and thirst for righteousness, for they will be filled. Blessed are the merciful, for they will be shown mercy. Blessed are the pure in heart, for they will see God. Blessed are the peacemakers, for they will be called children of God. Blessed are those who are persecuted because of righteousness, for theirs is the kingdom of heaven. Blessed are you when people insult you, persecute you and falsely say all kinds of evil against you because of me (Matthew 5:3-11) NIV.*

This scripture is all about those who are blessed. It also talks about how our core values, that is what is inside of us, reflects on what comes out of us in words and in actions. As Gary was talking about the different core values and the emotions they affect, I always seemed to be transfixed on one word in the diagram. That word was anger. As we were working our way around the circle of outward actions and getting closer to the topic of anger, I e-mailed Gary and told him that I had a "voice in my head" that was telling me I need to give my testimony about anger. Yes, I was asking to write up something and speak in front of people I did not know. This was and still is way out of my comfort zone and on a subject that is very painful for me. Since I do not speak up in class, this was of course a surprise to Gary, but he was also very appreciative of my stepping out in faith and out of my comfort zone to do this. A few weeks went by and we finally reached the topic of anger. We had things worked out as to how we would work my testimony into his teaching. He asked the class "who has had issues with anger?" Amazingly, I was the only one who raised my hand. I guess no one wanted to admit they had this problem. Which I can understand. Admitting something like this to others is very uncomfortable and humbling. I stood up and read my testimony. It was very difficult, and I had to choke back tears. After I finished reading it, one person came up to me and gave me a hug. We both cried and I think there were others that shed tears. Gary asked the class to comment on what I had just shared. One person in class said she remembered me back when I first started going to Hanfield. She said that the way I came across was very negative and she did not want to interact with me. In a way, this was upsetting, but at the same time, I completely understood why someone would not want to interact with me. My body language said I was a negative and angry person. After class, several people came up to me and thanked me. I can also remember at different times through life, people would ask me if I was ok, or ask if I was mad at something. I wasn't consciously mad at anything. But anger and negativity were showing on my face. I had never realized that.

This was a very humbling experience. I never really thought of myself as someone that might be able to help others with a problem that I have experience with or have overcome. I'm not one to tell a lot of people what is going on inside of me, let alone something so personal as my anger issues and the incidents that triggered it. A few months later, Gary asked me to give my testimony again at a Celebrate Recovery meeting. Only this time it had to last twenty minutes. This means talking in front of people longer than I had to the first time, and most likely to people I do not know at all and having to add more to my testimony. I did it. God did it. This is something so far out of my comfort zone that I cannot describe it. God is good. He helped me to not only expand my original testimony, but also get me through speaking in front of another group of people again. This time, there were people I knew and people I had never met before.

Some of you reading this may remember learning about the Sermon on the Mount and the Beatitudes in your Sunday school class. Some of you may know nothing about it. I vaguely remember hearing about it. But did not know or remember anything about it at all.

I'd like to share what I learned from my ABF class. I have been given permission to use this diagram and the teaching. As you can see, Anger is included with Murder.

Sermon on the Mount

- Fulfill law
- Salt/light
- Persecution
- Practice
- Murder/anger
- Fruit identifies
- Adultery/lust
- Narrow/wide
- Divorce
- Ask, seek, knock
- Oaths
- Beatitudes
- Don't judge
- No Revenge
- Don't worry
- Love enemies
- Treasures
- Give secretly
- Fast secretly
- Pray secretly

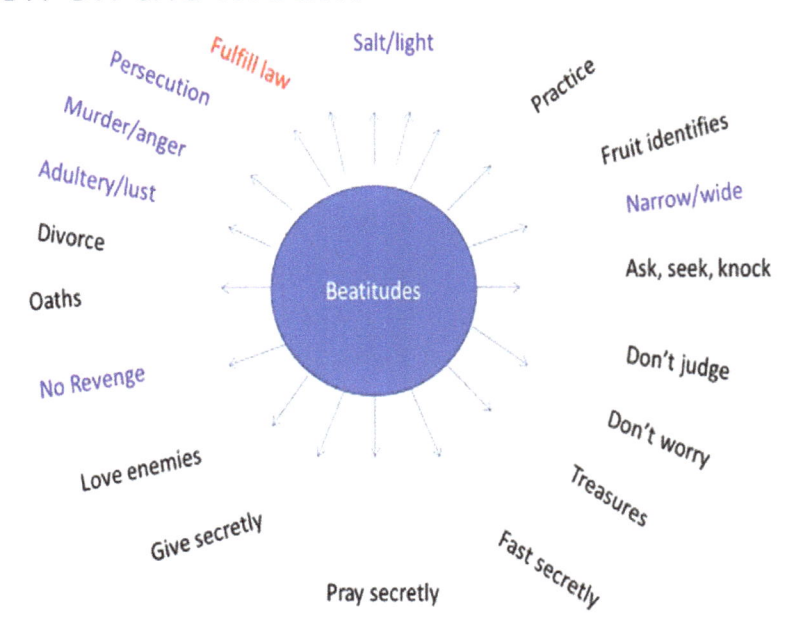

In the center of this diagram, you see the word "Beatitudes". These are found in the **Gospel of Matthew, Chapter 5** in the Bible. These are our core values. Depending on what our core values are makes a big difference on our outward actions, which are the words around the circle. If our core values are negative, then negativity comes out in our actions and words. But if our core values are positive, then positive comes out. Looking at the outward actions, what do you see that might be telling you what your core values are?

The Beatitudes from (**Matthew 5:3-9**) **NIV** are:

> *Blessed are the poor in spirit,*
> *for theirs is the kingdom of heaven.*
> *Blessed are those who mourn,*
> *for they will be comforted.*
> *Blessed are the meek,*
> *for they will inherit the earth.*
> *Blessed are those who hunger and thirst for righteousness,*
> *for they will be filled.*
> *Blessed are the merciful,*
> *for they will be shown mercy.*
> *Blessed are the pure in heart,*
> *for they will see God.*
> *Blessed are the peacemakers,*
> *for they will be called children of God."*

From these verses, the core values we are to live by are:

Right Values
- **These values relate to submitting to Jesus.**
    1. **Hungry for God** – starving for Him
    2. **Hate our sin and repent** – confess our faults and change
    3. **Rely on God and trust Him** – consciously submit our lives to God and rely on His help
    4. **Hungry to know God's word and obey it** – learn about God and apply His word to our lives
    5. **Show Sympathy & Compassion** – good works, resources
    6. **Yoked to Jesus** – abide in Him, identity in Him, allow no others, not double-minded
    7. **Be a Peacemaker and Reconciler** – witness and tell others what God has done for us
    8. **Show Agape Love** – show it to everyone

Part of my testimony reads as follows relating to the above list of Right Values:

How could I be Hungry for God? I did not know what that was.

How could I Hate Sin? The anger was my everyday sin?

How could I Rely on God and Be Obedient to Him? It was all about me.

How could I Show Sympathy and Compassion? I thought I did, but was I really showing either one?

How could I be yoked to Jesus? I did not know what this was either.

How could I be a Peacemaker? I was the one that was the aggressor and started the battles.

How could I show Agape Love? I did not even love myself.

I thought I loved my friends. How could I and did I really? I put a mask on every day. The mask was also a falsehood to me. I thought I was fine, but I wasn't.

FORGIVENESS, GRACE AND MERCY

In the **Gospel of Mark**, he says,

> *And whenever you stand praying, forgive, if you have anything against anyone, so that your Father who is in heaven will also forgive you your offenses. But if you do not forgive, neither will your Father who is in heaven forgive your offenses (Mark 11:25-26) NASB.*

Have you ever thought about how you physically feel inside and how you emotionally feel about yourself? How you truly treat others? When I was in counseling, I got hit with the stark realization of how I had treated people in the past and how I was treating people at that time. I mentioned earlier how terribly I had treated my sister, Patti when we were growing up. I felt horrible and ashamed once I remembered this. How could I do this to my sister? Shortly after I had this realization, I called her to apologize and to tell her I was in counseling for anger. We both started crying. She forgave me and was glad I was getting help. There are others that I would like to apologize to, but since I do not know where they are, I can't. I also learned that I had to forgive myself for the things I had done. Yes, I had done things wrong to other people and to myself, and this means I also did wrong to God. This is because everyone is a child of God and whoever we wrong, we do wrong unto God also. But the biggest thing I had to learn and do was to forgive the people that had hurt me. I thought I had done this long ago. You can say you forgive, but unless you truly mean it from your heart, the words mean nothing. Could I forgive from my heart? God has forgiven me for all the things that I had asked for forgiveness. So, this meant I had to forgive those that did me wrong. We often think that forgiveness is for the person that did us wrong. It isn't. Forgiveness is for each one of us. Forgiveness helps us with the hurt. The person that did us wrong has to live with the realization for the rest of their lives that they did something wrong to someone. We will never forget what was done wrong to us, but we can forgive. Forgiveness is for us, not the person who wronged us.

Remember, while Christ was on the cross, He forgave those that were crucifying Him. In the *Gospel of Luke* Jesus said, **Father, forgive them, for they do not know what they are doing (Luke 23:34) NIV**. If He can forgive the people who beat him, tortured him, then hung Him on a cross and left Him there to die, then I should be able to forgive those that did wrong to me.

In order to get past the bullying, being molested and raped, not getting the love from my mom that I should have and being taken advantage of by "George" and "John" I had to forgive all of them. I can't do this in person, but I can tell God I forgive them. Forgiveness must be done from the heart and not just from my mouth. It has been amazing what forgiveness has done for me. It's been a huge weight lifted off and my heart was softened a little more and I understand God's love more.

Forgiveness is hard for us to do. God does it every day even when we don't deserve it; and **we do not deserve** His forgiveness. Because that is what God does. It's called Grace.

I looked up the definitions for convict, condemn, grace and forgiveness in the *Merriam Webster Dictionary* and found the following:

Convict:

having been convicted
to find or prove to be guilty
to convince of error or sinfulness

Condemn:

to declare to be reprehensible, wrong, or evil usually after weighing evidence and without reservation to pronounce guilty: convict sentence, doom (condemn a prisoner to die)

    Notice how the word convict is just saying that you did something wrong. But the definition of condemn not only includes the word convict, but also uses reprehensible, wrong, evil and doom. Condemnation is not from God it is from Satan but only after he lures us into doing something wrong. Conviction is that nudge you get from God saying you did wrong. I like to call it that "flea flick" upside my head.

Grace:

"unmerited divine assistance given to humans for their regeneration or sanctification"
"a virtue coming from God"
"a state of sanctification enjoyed through divine assistance"
"archaic: mercy, pardon"
"a special favor: privilege"
"disposition to or an act or instance of kindness, courtesy, or clemency"
"a temporary exemption: reprieve"

Forgiveness:

"the act of forgiving – I ask for your forgiveness"

"to cease to feel resentment against (an offender): pardon
"forgive one's enemies"
"to give up resentment of or claim to requital (see requital 1) for
"forgive an insult"

Grace and forgiveness are similar, but not completely alike. All of us say we forgive others. But, do we really mean it from the heart. Then there's forgiving ourselves. Do we do that? Not often enough or not at all. Have you ever thought about the fact that we also need to forgive ourselves for the wrong things we have done? We do. We may ask others to forgive us and they may. We ask God to forgive us, and HE WILL, with no strings attached. But do we forgive ourselves. It's hard to do because we feel guilty. As you may notice, the definition of grace is mostly about coming from God. If we ask, we will receive grace and mercy every day from God. But will others (humans) give us grace or mercy?

Here's what the *Merriam Webster Dictionary* says about **Mercy**:

"compassion or forbearance (see forbearance) shown especially to an offender or to one subject to one's power; also: lenient or compassionate treatment"

Forbearance: a refraining from the enforcement
of something that is due
the act of forbearing: patience
the quality of being forbearing: leniency

"imprisonment rather than death imposed as penalty for first-degree murder"
"a blessing that is an act of divine favor or compassion"
"a fortunate circumstance"
"compassionate treatment of those in distress"

Grace and mercy are more similar than they are to forgiveness. They are all given to those when it is not deserved. Humans are not so willing to do this, but God will give them all to us if we ask and if we are willing to receive them. We can learn to give grace, mercy, and forgiveness to those that do not deserve it. But we need to ask God to help us with this.

There is a song by Phillips Craig and Dean called "**Tell Your Heart to Beat Again.**" This song talks about forgiving ourselves, and letting go of the past. Here are the lyrics.

Forgiven
If only you'd forgive yourself
You've been made new
But you're standing where you fell
Because when you look in the mirror

It seems like all you ever see
Are the scars of every failure
And the you that you used to be

Tell your heart to beat again
Close your eyes and breathe it in
Let the shadows fall away
You'll live to love another day
Yesterday's a closing door
And you don't live there anymore
So say goodbye to where you've been
And tell your heart to beat again

Forgiven
Just let that word wash over you
It's all right now
Love's healing hands have pulled you through
So, get back up and take step one
And now your new life has begun
And know that if the Son has set you free
Then you are free indeed!

Tell your heart to beat again
Close your eyes and breathe it in
Let the shadows fall away
You'll live to love another day
Yesterday's a closing door
And you don't live there anymore
So say goodbye to where you've been

And tell your heart to beat again

Hope is reaching from a rugged cross
Where a perfect love recaptured all the innocence that's lost
And mercy's calling from an empty grave
So life your eyes to heaven
And hear your Savior say

Tell your heart to beat again
Close your eyes and breathe it in
Let the shadows fall away
You'll live to love another day
Yesterday's a closing door
And you don't live there anymore
So say goodbye to where you've been
And tell your heart to beat again

Songwriters: Matthew West/Bernie Herms/Randy Phillips

Tell Your Heart to Beat Again lyrics © Warner/Chappell Music, Inc, Universal Music Publishing Group, Capitol Christian Music Group

This song came out a few years after I was released from counselling, but it has played a big part in my life. It is a constant reminder not to live or dwell in the past. We can look at the past to see how far we have come, but do not linger there. It does us no good. We can't change the past. When we have been verbally and emotionally abused, there's a recording that keeps playing in our minds. It tells us that we are no good and won't amount to anything. This is just Satan's way of trying to keep us down in his world. Yes, a person said those things to us and may also have said to not tell anyone. But not telling anyone keeps us in the dark and Satan likes the dark. God tells us we are good, and God is the light. Satan cannot survive in the light. Once we get those words and recordings out of our minds and into the light, those things cannot hurt us anymore. It's freedom!

There is a song by Tenth Avenue North called "Losing" that also talks about forgiveness and grace. Asking God to forgive those that have hurt us because they may not know what they are doing to us. This is what Christ did while on the cross. **"Jesus said, "Father, forgive them, for they do not know what they are doing..." (Luke 23:34) NIV**.

Christ was being crucified, yet He still asked God to forgive everyone for what they had done to Him. The song says we need to ask God to give us the grace to forgive those that have hurt us because we feel like we are the ones that are losing and not them.

RUNNING AND ENDURANCE

We need to have God in our lives to help us through everything and all the everyday issues that go on. There's another scripture that means a lot to me and speaks to us needing God in our lives.

The apostle Paul says,

> *"I can do all things through Christ who strengthens me" (Philippians.4:13) NKJV.*

The world we live in tells us that we can do everything by ourselves. Me, myself, and I is what "the world" says. Whatever we can get, we get through our own strength. Unfortunately, this will lead us straight to Hell. This is the difference between the wide and the narrow paths that are talked about in the Bible.

Christ talks about the wide and narrow gates. He says,

> **"Go in through the narrow door. The door is wide and the road is easy that leads to hell. Many people are going through that door. But the door is narrow and the road is hard that leads to life that lasts forever. Few people are finding it" (Matthew 7:13-14) NLV.**

We need to find the narrow road and narrow gate if we expect to get into heaven to live an everlasting life with Christ and God. That road and gate is to accept Christ as our Lord and Savior and to serve Him. It will not be easy, but God will be with us always.

At age of fifty-two, I took up running. I had been challenged by someone at work to participate in a 5k, which is 3.1 miles. Since I had never been a runner, I walked most of it. It took me about fifty-one minutes to complete, but after that I was hooked. I started training on my own without having any idea as to how to do this. First with some running/walking on the treadmill at the YMCA. Then I would run/walk in 5k races on the weekends. Even though I wasn't training formally, I was doing well at it. Then someone at Hanfield found online a "couch to 5k" style of training that combined Bible study with training to run a 5k. It's called Run for God. The scripture used as the foundation for Run for God is:

"Therefore, since we are surrounded by such a great cloud of witnesses, let us throw off everything that hinders and the sin that so easily entangles. And let us run with perseverance the race marked out for us" **(Hebrews 12:1) NIV.**

It's amazing how much endurance and perseverance is tied to running. These are also a must in seeking God and His Word. It took perseverance and a form of endurance for me to continue with counselling for thirteen years, to learn how to run, and to study the Bible. We must be reading and studying the Bible every day. The more we are reading and studying the Bible, the closer we get to God. He created us in His image. He wants us to be a part of Him. He wants us to want Him.

The enemy or Satan wants to keep us away from God's word. Satan is the great liar. He twists the truth to suit his own agenda, which is to have us separate ourselves from God. And it all started in the Garden of Eden when Satan twisted the truth of what God told Adam and Eve. God told them to not to eat or touch the fruit of the tree in the center of the garden. If they did, they would die. Satan twisted this truth. Satan told Eve that they would not die, but that their eyes would be open, and they would be like God. And, because they disobeyed, they were sent out of the garden and thus sin was born. What died was their soul and the good life they had. God does give us free will. But we must use it wisely. Unfortunately, we tend to use this free will to serve ourselves and our sin nature. Staying in God's word can be a powerful weapon against spiritual warfare and keep our hearts and minds focused on God.

When it comes to my past anger issues, it took a lot of perseverance and endurance to press through to get past it. To relive the pain and hurt in my heart and soul. A few months into my counseling, I had the thought to just not go anymore. My thinking was telling me that it was not working. Not helping me any. I was not getting any better. I was still angry. What I was going to do was not call and cancel the appointment, I was just not going to show up anymore. Satan was controlling my thinking. At the time, I finally admitted I had anger issues, it had been many years since most of what had happened to me. Things normally don't happen overnight. They take time to manifest. Therefore, it was going to take time and God's help to get past my anger. **"For the word of God is quick, and powerful, and sharper than any two-edged sword, piercing even to the dividing asunder of soul and spirit, and of the joints and marrow, and is a discerner of the thoughts and intents of the heart" (Hebrews 4:12) KJV**. Staying in the word helps you combat the enemy and stay focused on the right path.

MY BAPTISM, INNER PEACE AND THE NEW BATTLE

Once a year in August, Hanfield had an outdoor baptism at a pond that is at the home of one of the parishioners. The baptism is done by submersion. Oh, before I go any further, I need to tell you I had been baptized when I was in the ninth or tenth grade. This was because I was to be confirmed into the church I attended at that time. But because I had not been baptized, I had to be baptized first. So, it was just a means to an end. It had to be done if I wanted to be confirmed. Now back to what I started. Every year they would announce this starting a couple of months prior to the Baptism. In 2007, I had a "Voice" in my head that was telling me "you need to do this". This voice persisted. I had no idea at the time it was God's voice. My response "to myself" every time was "I don't like being the center of attention". The outdoor baptism came and went. In 2008, this "Voice" again said to me "you need to do this". Again, I didn't listen and said "to myself" "I don't like being the center of attention". Again, the baptism came and went. In 2009, it was a completely different story. I got the "Voice" in my head again saying, "you need to do this." Once again, I said "to myself" "I don't like being the center of attention." No sooner had that thought gone through my head, the voice of God said to me "It's not about you." Wow! This was a huge wakeup call. It was not just a passing thought in my head. It was God telling me I needed to be baptized. God really knows how to get our attention when we don't listen to Him or when we just say no when He wants us to do something. This time I did go through with the baptism, and it was a beautiful experience. But I cannot describe the feeling I had after it. The Holy Spirit was truly there. One thing I do remember is when Pastor Tim asked, for someone to be first, no one moved. Then I was the one that stepped up. Yes, the one that said, "I don't like being the center of attention." I had invited my friend Debbie, her husband Tim and my counsellor, Bonnie. They had been through everything with me. Deb had seen some of my anger too. When I came out of the water, I just started crying. I was overwhelmed by what I was feeling. I went under the water as one person and came out feeling like a completely different person. I felt like everything had been washed away. All the anger, anxiety, and guilt. This is what baptism is. Washing away the old person and coming out as a new person. Burying the sin.

The apostle Paul writes:

> *Or have you forgotten that when we were joined with Christ Jesus in baptism, we joined him in his death? For we died and were buried with Christ by baptism. And just as Christ was raised from the dead by the glorious power of the Father, now we also may live new lives.* **(Romans 6:3-4) NLT.**

ANGER RAGE DANGER

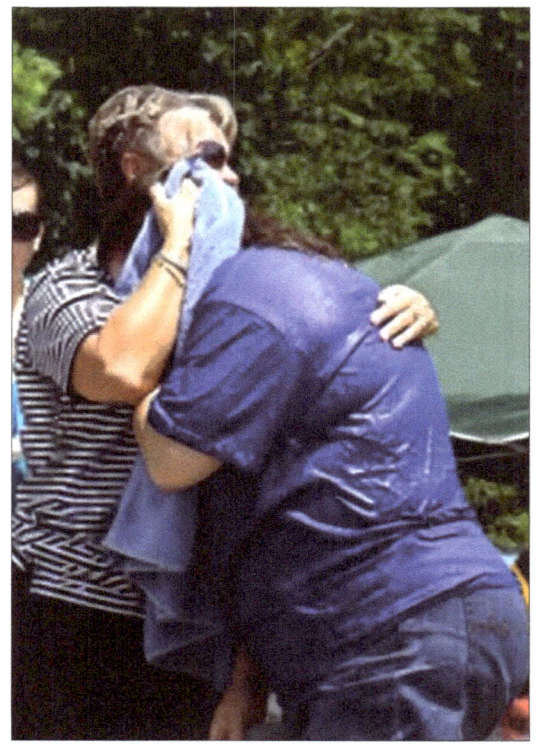

God's timing is a lot different than ours. A few months after I was baptized, Bonnie released me from counselling. I wonder how much things would have changed in my life if I had only listened to the "Voice" two years before. I don't dwell on that because I cannot change the past. I can learn from it and do my best not to repeat it. But I do periodically look back to see how far I have come. Also, if I had listened the first time, would I be writing this book?

After I had been baptized, I was now nearing the end of counseling, which at the time I obviously did not realize. I remember the last few sessions I had with Bonnie. We always started just by chatting before we got down to business. I remember her asking me how I was doing. I told her I just felt blah. This was not the sick kind of blah; it was just a nothing feeling I had. This went on for a few sessions. She knew what was going on, but I didn't. She was trying to get me to realize what it was I was feeling. So, the last time this happened, she asked me if what I was feeling was peace. WOW!! That was it!! Peace inside of me!! I had never felt this way before, so I did not recognize it. I felt peace. Then realized there was happiness and joy inside my heart and soul. I had never felt these feelings before. At different times, I would be happy, but it was not the same as these feelings. But this meant a "bigger battle" was about to start. Once she helped me realize what I was feeling, I started to have two competing voices in my head. These voices were God and Satan. Satan's voice was saying "you shouldn't be feeling this way." But God was right there telling me, "Yes you should be feeling this way." This battle went on for a long time. But over time, this battle gradually faded with God's voice winning and my feeling good and the voice telling me I shouldn't feel that way was gone. I now know that I should feel happiness, joy, and peace. There are times though when these feelings are not there. And that's ok. We all have those days. And when we do, God is there with me to help me through the troubles.

Another song that came out about three years after my counselling ended is by Hillsong United, called **Cornerstone**. This song tells us that Christ needs to be the Cornerstone in our lives. Here are those lyrics:

My hope is built on nothing less
Than Jesus' blood and righteousness
I dare not trust the sweetest frame
But holly trust is Jesus' name

My hope is built on nothing less
Than Jesus' blood and righteousness
I dare not trust the sweetest frame
But holly trust is Jesus' name

Christ alone, Cornerstone
Weak made strong in the Savior's love
Through the storm
He is Lord
Lord of all

When darkness seems to hide His face
I rest on His unchanging grace
In every high and stormy gale
My anchor holds within the veil
My anchor holds within the veil

Christ alone, Cornerstone
Weak made strong in the Savior's love
Through the storm
He is Lord
Lord of all
He is Lord
Lord of all, Christ alone

Christ alone, Cornerstone
Weak made strong in the Savior's love
Through the storm
He is Lord
Lord of all

Christ alone, Cornerstone
Weak made strong in the Savior's love
Through the storm

He is Lord
Lord of all
When he shall come with trumpet sound
Oh, may I then in Him be found
Dressed in His righteousness alone
Faultless, stand before the throne

Cornerstone
Oh, yeah, in the Savior's love
He is Lord
Lord of all

Christ alone, Cornerstone
Weak made strong in the Savior's love
Through the storm
He is Lord
Lord of all

Songwriters: Eric Liljero / Jonas Myrin / Reuben Morgan

Cornerstone lyrics © Capitol Christian Music Group

    Every time I would hear this song, I would cry. Realizing how much God and Christ had done for me and that He needs to always be the Cornerstone in my life and in your life. In all aspects of my life and in all aspects of your life. Without Him I would not be who I am.

God does talk to us, but we usually aren't listening. We have a Voice in our head that says we should be happy. This is God. We also have a Voice in our head that says we shouldn't do something if the outcome will be bad. This is God. He knows the outcome before we do. Then there's Satan's voice that says go ahead and do this. It usually is not a good thing. Satan twists things to make this not good thing look like something that there won't be any consequences. This is usually followed by God's voice telling us to not do it and that there will be consequences. If we go ahead and do what we shouldn't have done, Satan is usually right there to tell us "you shouldn't have done that." Satan condemns us after the fact. He is the great liar. God will convict us of the wrongdoing but will not condemn us. If we do something wrong God will still love us and will let the consequences fall on us. All we must do now is ask God to forgive us and we have to not do it again. If we truly mean it, God will forgive us AND forget what we did. But God also knows that we will still do wrong and loves us anyway. No matter how many times we sin. He Will Always Love Us.

> **"Therefore, there is now no condemnation for those who are in Christ Jesus" (Romans 8:1) NIV.**

As I am writing this book, I have been looking back to all the good things that were happening and seeing that Satan was trying to keep me from accomplishing the good things. Wanting to not continue the counseling was Satan trying to tell me it was not doing any good. Satan wanted to keep me angry. Like I said, it was early in my counseling, and this was a great time for Satan to twist the truth to get me to stop. Especially since Bonnie was a Christian counselor and Satan knew this. Satan was trying to take me as his captive and keep me there. Angry and feeling hopeless. But I persevered and did end up keeping that appointment and every appointment after that for thirteen years. There's a couple of sayings that come to mind. "It is darkest before the dawn." The other is "things will get worse before they get better." Yes, my anger did get worse before it got better. The incident I mentioned about going into a rage at a bar was after about a year of not going to counseling. Once that happened, I called Bonnie, went back to counseling, and did not stop going until she released me. The reason I did not go for about a year was due to my obtaining my truck driving license (CDL). Yes, I did suffer a little longer, but it finally got better, and I have the kind of peace and happiness that God wants for me and for everyone.

BULLIED & MOLESTED

The bullying I experienced when I was growing up was not much different than what you see today. Except, there was no internet to keep things going. Kids as well as adults now put this stuff on the internet to bully others. I wonder if these people would be doing the bullying if there was no internet. This form of bullying means no physical contact with those they choose to bully. Using the internet for bullying means the person being the bully isn't going to get physically hurt but has power and can stay hidden. This is what Satan loves. He wants things hidden in darkness.

When I was a kid, I was teased verbally by the boys in elementary school and in my neighborhood because I was overweight and had buckteeth. Not only did these boys follow me home, but one would punch me or dig his knuckle into my back in class because he knew the teacher could not see what he was doing. One time, this same boy was doing this to me in the lunch line. I don't remember how things all transpired, but I must have been crying and we were both taken to the principal's office. I wouldn't say anything as to what was going on. I certainly didn't want it to get worse if he got into trouble. However, because I didn't say anything, it didn't get any better either. These boys would also throw eggs at the house at night and hopefully get away before my dad could get out to catch them. All of this happened in elementary school. By the time junior high came around, I guess they had grown up enough that they did not bully me anymore. What's funny is that I do have contact with one of my tormentors. As the saying goes, "getting older is mandatory, growing up is optional."

 Being molested and raped was horrific. I think what made it worse is that it was a neighbor that I would see a lot. I had no one I could tell. At that time, I didn't know why, but I finally realized in counseling why I couldn't tell anyone. My mom had led me to believe that anything that happened to me was my fault. This all started with just touching. He asked me if I wanted to see his hunting dogs. He took me into the kennel where the dogs were kept. It was large and semi enclosed. This was just a lure to get me into a place that no one could see what he would do. I knew it was wrong, but I didn't know what to do. What's even scarier is that I remember it felt both good and bad. Saying it felt good is extremely embarrassing to say. But I also knew and felt that it was wrong. I just stood there and let him do what he wanted. The next time I went to babysit for them on a Saturday, he came home at lunchtime. He had gone upstairs for something. He then called me upstairs. Unbeknownst to me, he was planning to do much more to me. He started touching and kissing me. The next thing I knew he had me on the bed and was trying to have sex with me. No, I stand corrected. He was trying to rape me. I was only about twelve years old. He was over six feet tall and very muscular. His girls were under five years old. I knew this was wrong, but I couldn't say anything. I couldn't cry out. I just closed my eyes so I could not see him. I just laid there and hoped it would be over soon. I was very lucky that nothing really happened to me that day. This unfortunately continued every time I babysat for them. I wanted to earn my own money and babysitting was the way to do it back then. I would pray every weekend that he would not take his lunch break at the house and that I would be free from his abuse. Unfortunately, he would take his lunch break at the house. What's unfortunate is that when I got older, and finally wanted to have charges brought against him, I couldn't. I was too old, and it wasn't a repressed memory that was suddenly remembered. However, I have forgiven him, but I have never forgotten what he did.

Something this possibly caused later, was that I became very promiscuous in college and after college. I let guys take advantage of me, sexually, emotionally, verbally, and financially. I don't know if I couldn't or just didn't want to say no because I wanted to be in a relationship with someone.

Now, I want you to understand that the first boyfriend I had "Carl," did none of these things. He was a wonderful person and treated me great. I never told him of what happened when I was a child. The older we got it was me that did not treat him very well. When I would pick fights, I never got physical with him. I would just yell and scream.

THE BIG PICTURE AND GOD'S PLAN

What we don't realize is that God sees the big picture. He knows how our lives will turn out. He gives us free will, which is why we sin. He knows if things in our lives happen a certain way, we will go down a certain path. Since we have free will, we can change this. Unfortunately, because of the way I was brought up and the things that happened to me as a child caused me to have a difficult life. When I was in my twenties, I was thinking I would be married to my high school sweetheart, "Carl", and have a family. At the start of writing this book, I was about fifty-five years old, have never been married and do not have a family. God knew that I would not have been a good wife and mother. There are days I'm disappointed and sad that I'm still single. Yes, it would be nice to come home to someone, have someone to talk to at night or just sit with. But the flip side to that is, if I want to go out and do something, I do not have to run it by my spouse. I can just go.

My friends may or may not know that I'm a very shy and insecure person. I am not very outgoing and still uncomfortable around people I do not know.

God knows this and has done a lot of things to pull me out of my comfort zone. As I mentioned before, I was baptized at a pond in front of a lot of people. Oh, yeah. I was the first one to step up to be baptized. I've spoken in front of the congregation at Hanfield Church three different times, in front of my ABF class twice, and in front of a Celebrate Recovery group twice. The next thing that God had me do was to take part in the giving of Communion at Hanfield. This doesn't involve speaking to a large crowd all at once, but it does involve saying something to each person that takes the bread and the juice. I haven't mentioned this anyone including my ABF group. But they will find out tomorrow. There were two more times I spoke in front of people. At this writing I am now living back on the east coast, in Maine. When I was leaving Hanfield, Pastor Tim asked if it would be ok during both services to pray for me. I said, "yes." I then asked if I could say something before he prayed for me. Yes, I was nervous, but Hanfield meant so much to me in my growth and walk with God that I had to say good-bye publicly.

    I mentioned earlier that I lived with a married couple for a while before I lived in Indiana. It's obvious now, but I do remember at that time I contemplated committing suicide. I was going to slit my wrists. What saved me was that the scissors were dull. They didn't even put a scratch on me. That got me to thinking about counseling. I sought out someone but was not comfortable with the person I spoke with. He also told me the person that went with me was doing the same thing for me that the counselor would do, but for free. Well, that person ended up not doing anything for me after that and I had a lot of problems that went on for years.

"To all who mourn in Israel, he will give a crown of beauty for ashes, a joyous blessing instead of mourning, festive praise instead of despair. In their righteousness, they will be like great oaks that the Lord has planted for his own glory" (Isaiah 61:3) NLT.

I was in the ashes and did not think highly of myself. Not knowing it at the time, that recording was playing in my head. I'm not pretty. I won't be worth anything. I'm a failure. But God!!! God thinks of all of us as his children. We have been given beauty for ashes if we will just receive it and accept it. But we must listen to (and for) Him. If we are not listening, we cannot receive all the gifts and beauty he wants to bestow on us. Yes, beauty is what we see, but it is also what we are inside if we would just take the time to receive it. It's what's inside that comes out as to how we treat others. We tend to only see the physical beauty. God sees the beauty in our heart.

Recently I moved back to the east coast from Indiana, which meant leaving a job that I had been at for almost sixteen years. I attribute my decision to move to God prompting me earlier in the year. The prompting was to help my sister with the day - to - day things concerning our mom who was in a memory care facility. The day I was to leave Indiana, I remembered I had not looked at the daily Bible verse that comes to me each day through a text message from WBCL. When I opened it up, the verse was so appropriate for the situation into which I was going. It read:

> **For I know the plans I have for you, declares the Lord, plans to prosper you and not to harm you, plans to give you hope and a future. (Jeremiah 29:11) NIV.**

Ever since I retired from the bank, I have felt such peace and I have not been anxious at all. The only way this could be is because of God in my life. He was with me through my 1,200-mile drive. My drive gave me a lot of time to think and talk with God. Not necessarily praying, but just talking. As I mentioned before, He wants a relationship with us.

There were a couple of situations that could have been a lot different if God hadn't been with me. As I got closer to the East Coast, I was finding that drivers had not really changed much from what I remembered, very impatient and aggressive. If I had not become a changed person with God's help, I would have fallen right back into the anger trap in which I worked so hard and for many years to get away from. I didn't let my anger get the better of me. As a matter of fact, I was not worried or anxious at all during the many miles I had to go. If someone got impatient with me, I just kept doing what I was doing (so long as it was not wrong) and let that person go around me.

Anger and rage will not take us anywhere good. Rage and the wrong kind of anger will just get us into trouble. They both result from a hard heart, which will cause us to be unable to show true love to others. If we are angry and have a hard heart, we cannot even love ourselves. I never understood the phrase "having a hard heart" until I was "fixed," so to say. It is something that can be felt, but I couldn't feel that my heart was hard until it had been softened. Once my heart was softened, I didn't know what I was feeling because I had never felt that way before. My counselor, Bonnie had to tell me that I finally had peace. Then I understood what I was feeling.

God talks of replacing a hard heart with a softened heart and His Spirit in the following scripture from Ezekiel:

> *I will give you a new heart and put a new spirit in you; I will remove from you your heart of stone and give you a heart of flesh. And I will put my Spirit in you and move you to follow my*

decrees and be careful to keep my laws. (Ezekiel 36:26-27) NIV.

Another scripture I ran across that is appropriate for my transition is the following:

So do not fear, for I am with you;
  do not be dismayed, for I am your God.
I will strengthen you and help you;
  I will uphold you with my righteous right hand.
(Isaiah 41:10) NIV.

We should not be afraid of change. Change can sometimes make us angry because we want to stay in our comfort zone. Change means our comfort zone will temporarily be uncomfortable. Our comfort zone will come back, but it will be after the change has settled in. It will be a new comfort zone. Then if God feels we have been in the new comfort zone too long, He might start prompting us to change again. The longer we stay angry at something or someone, the harder it will be to settle into the new environment.

False
Evidence
Appearing
Real

Fear is what Satan uses with us. When someone molests you and tells you "don't tell anyone, it will be our secret," this is actually Satan. If someone rapes you and tells you to not tell anyone because they will hurt your family, that is also Satan instilling fear into us. If we keep the wrongs to ourselves, it's like keeping them in the dark and Satan likes being in the dark. Satan cannot live or thrive in the light. The light is God's Goodness. The light can and will overcome the darkness. As a child, when I was molested and then raped, I do not recall being told to keep it to myself. But I knew I could not tell anyone what was happening. This was because of "what I had been led to believe" by my mom. That the things that happened to me were my fault. But not in those exact words. However, that was what I understood as a child when I'd come home from school crying after being bullied by the kids at and after school. It was "my fault" I was being bullied or teased. Of course, I learned much later in counseling that anything like this is not my (or your) fault. It is also what you should believe. It is NOT your fault. Yes, it is hard to tell someone this type of thing is happening. My dad and I were very close and talked about just about anything. But I couldn't tell him about this. He passed away in 2003 and never knew.

What actually makes things like this even more troublesome is that after I had been in counseling for a while, I contacted the state of Massachusetts to find out if I could go after "Robert" for molesting and raping me. Mind you I was in my thirties at that point. I didn't want money, I just wanted to see that he "paid" for what he did. I was told that since the incident was not a repressed memory that I had all of a sudden remembered and because it was too many years after I turned 18, there was nothing I could do. This was and is appalling. My concern is that "Robert" may have done it to others. We say that people that commit this type of act are "sick." There are some, that have some kind of mental illness. But there are those that are not "sick." Although it is sick to do this to a child. But Satan is working in them to keep the depravity in this world going. The innocent children that must suffer from being abused and molested needs to stop. If we all start by praying and asking God to help us help them, things can change. If I had not gone through what I went through, I would not be writing this book. So, it all goes back to:

> **And we know that all things work together for good to those who love God, to those who are the called according to His purpose (Romans 8:28) NKJV**

Bad things did happen to me for many years of my life. But if they had not happened, I would not be the person I am today. I had once been asked, if there was something you could change in your life, what would it be? My answer was everything. A few years later that question popped into my head again. In our ABF group, Gary would give us a scripture verse every week to study. This time it was *Romans 8:28*. The following week Gary would ask us if we had anything to say regarding the verse or if we had an experience with God. One of the few times I spoke up in class was this time. I mentioned the original question from years earlier. "If I could change something in my life, what would it be?" This time I realized that there would be absolutely nothing I would change. If I could change something, then I would not be the person that I am today.

God **never** makes a mistake. God is everywhere and knows everything. He did not make a mistake when He made you or me. If you are hearing in your head that you are not worthwhile or that you will never amount to anything, that is **not** God. That is Satan trying to get you or someone else to follow him or trying to get you to think less of yourself. This worked for me for a lot of years. But then once I found Christ I realized that I am not the person that won't amount to anything. When you were born, you were put on this earth or a purpose. We cannot see the big picture. God knows the reason He created each one of us. I do not know what my purpose is here on earth. Maybe I was put here so I could tell my story of abuse, anger, and depression and how I came out on the other side a much better and stronger person.

Only God knows why. If what I write, can help just one person, then that is why I was put on this earth. If it helps more than that, then that is great. I may never know if this helps someone overcome anger and depression. This may be something that I will find out only when I make it to heaven.

THE "RECORDING" IN MY HEAD

This morning, I was reminded with a song by Lauren Dagle that talks about these voices in our head. They sometimes tell us we are not worthy and that we won't be any good. This is the voice of Satan. God will **not** condemn us. He will **not** tell us we are no good. We are worthy and we are good. We are loved. We are strong. God is with us and always holds on to us. We need to cling to what God thinks of us and not what the world tells us we are. God is only truth. Satan is nothing but lies.

I keep coming back to my having been teased and bullied. Today I was also reminded of a saying, "Sticks and stones may break my bones, but words will never hurt me." Yes, our bones can physically break, but they will heal. Unlike what the saying says, words do hurt. They hurt in our soul and in our heart. Because as a child I was led to believe that everything was my fault, it ended up that I did believe it. Even though I was called names because of how I looked, it hurt. But, "it was my fault." Being punched, kicked, and bullied, hurt physically and mentally but "it was my fault" the boys were doing this. All this leads to a low self-esteem. I didn't realize I had low self-esteem until counseling. Then I got to thinking. Whenever someone would complement me, I always managed to turn it into a negative. If someone complimented me on an outfit I was wearing, if it was an older outfit, I would say something like, "oh, this old thing?". I would always find ways to turn a positive into a negative. I had to learn to, just say "thank you." I can remember at one point I was having some financial difficulty and asked to borrow some money from a co-worker. She was happy to do it. This was ok. But if someone offered to lend (or give) me some money, I would often turn it down. This leads back to something else I had issues with…control. If I asked for a loan, I was in control. If someone offered me money, I was not in control.

Control issues are often born out of the kind of issues I had, from being bullied and molested. Having control means that I will not let anyone ever control me again. The problem is we don't have control. We think we do, but we really don't. We put up a wall around us, or around our heart, so no one can be let in and then we won't get hurt again. But what this does is it also keeps us from experiencing God's Love and what He's trying to say to us. There are still days when I don't hear God's voice. But I try to listen more and more every day. Although, listening and hearing God's voice is all well and good, but we then must acknowledge and receive what He is saying. I must give up control to have faith and trust in God.

GOD'S LOVE, ANGER AND PUNISHMENT

God is good. God is patient. But God does get angry. However, His anger is righteous, unlike our anger. Our anger is usually far from being righteous. It almost always is sinful. In **Genesis 3** is the first time we see God get angry. He was angry due to Adam and Eve doing what they were told not to do. They ate the fruit from the tree God specifically told them not to eat. But God did give them free will. Adam blamed Eve and Eve blamed the serpent. And this is what we tend to do. We tend to blame someone else for what we did that was wrong. The punishment was that Adam and Eve were sent out of Eden.

> To the woman he said, "I will make your pains in childbearing very severe; with painful labor you will give birth to children. Your desire will be for your husband, and he will rule over you." To Adam he said, "Because you listened to your wife and ate fruit from the tree about which I commanded you, 'You must not eat from it, "Cursed is the ground because of you; through painful toil you will eat food from it all the days

of your life. It will produce thorns and thistles for you, and you will eat the plants of the field. By the sweat of your brow you will eat your food until you return to the ground, since from it you were taken; for dust you are and to dust you will return (Genesis 3: 16-19) NIV.

From that point on, God also caused the serpent to crawl on its belly. God also blocked the Garden of Eden so no one would be able to get to the tree of life.

In **Genesis 19**, is the story of Sodom and Gomorrah. Here is another example of when God had had enough of our sin nature and brings his judgment. The only people in Sodom that God did not destroy were Lot and his family. But because of the sins that were committed by everyone else in Sodom and Gomorrah, God destroyed these cities.

The last story I will tell of God's righteous anger is also in *Genesis*. In **Genesis 6**, the story of Noah. Humans in the world had become so corrupt and full of sin. God regretted creating humans and decided he would destroy the world including animals to start over. The only exception was Noah and his family.

So, the Lord was sorry he had ever made them and put them on the earth. It broke his heart. And the Lord said, "I will wipe this human race I have created from the face of the earth. Yes, and I will destroy every living thing-all the people,

the large animals, the small animals that scurry along the ground, and even the birds of the sky. I am sorry I ever made them." But Noah found favor with the Lord. (Genesis 6:6-8) NLT

Jesus being human also became angry. But unlike us, his anger was also righteous as opposed to how our anger normally is realized. This is found in **Matthew 21** where Jesus overturned the tables in the temple due to the corruption of the money changers and those that bought and sold animals for sacrifice. Here is what the gospel says:

Jesus entered the temple courts and drove out all who were buying and selling there. He overturned the tables of the money changers and the benches of those selling doves. It is written, he said to them, My house will be called a house of prayer, but you are making it a den of robbers. (Matthew 21:12-13) NIV

GIVE IT TO GOD

The Bible has a lot of scriptures that speak about anger and being angry. There's a saying that we use frequently. "Do not let the sun go down on your anger." This is found in **Ephesians 4**. But, this is only part of what is written. Here is what Paul writes:

> *In your anger do not sin. Do not let the sun go down while you are still angry, and do not give the devil a foothold. (Ephesians 4:26-27)* **NIV**

If we let anger stay with us while we are sleeping, the devil already has a head start on us for the next morning. If I am angry when I am ready for bed, I try to remember to ask God to take it from me so, I can have a peaceful sleep.

Yes, I do still get angry. Hopefully, I'm no longer sinning with my anger. You might wonder, how am I sinning when I get angry. One way your anger would be a sin is breaking out in a rage. Screaming and yelling when it's not necessary. Chasing someone down the road in your car so you could do to that person what they had done to you. Both are using your anger in a sinful way. Righteous anger is when you just give the anger over to God, pray, and if possible, just discuss the issue with the person you're angry with. This does not always feel good. It's hard to discuss an issue peacefully with the one that has hurt you. I have found that when I do get angry, I have not felt the rage that I used to feel. When someone does something stupid on the road, I no longer want to chase that person down the road and treat that person the same way they treated me. I just say to myself "Oh well, hopefully, you don't take anyone out with that behavior."

When I talk on the phone at work, and I talk with someone who really irritates me, I must consciously tell myself to let it go when I get off the phone. Sometimes I remember to do this, and sometimes I don't. I actually have a three-by-five-inch card that hangs at my desk which says, "Give it to God." I also have one in my car that says the same thing. It's always a reminder to me to let it go. Only God can do what we cannot. If we give it to Him, He will take care of things for us. We are always thinking we can do everything on our own, but we cannot. If you think about it, God already knows how each of our lives will turn out. He sees and knows "the big picture." He knows that if we obey Him, our lives will turn out one way. He also knows where our lives will end up if we go down that "wide road." He loves all of us and is always with us, calling us back to Him. Most of the time, we are not even listening to that "little Voice" in our heads. Depending on the circumstance, when we hear that voice, we just pass it off as being paranoid. That voice is also a voice that can save our lives if we listen and do what it is saying. Earlier, I mentioned that when I was in college, I had become promiscuous and smoked pot. At one of the schools, I was at, a friend of one of the people I was smoking with, offered me a pill. I had no idea what it was. What I do remember was that something (Someone) was telling me not to take it. I did not try it and am probably glad I didn't. There was probably that same Voice telling me not to drink, smoke pot and not to be promiscuous. But I didn't listen then. Every time, the Voice was God. At least I'm fine. I travel an hour each way to and from work every day. There have been times, especially in bad weather, when there's that little Voice telling me to either turn around and go a different way or to leave earlier or later. Inevitably, later that day or the next day or two I will hear about an accident or incident that happened on the road I was, (or would have been), on. The timing was such that if I had continued, I probably would have been involved.

To wrap things up, I lived most of my life a very angry person. I was also depressed and did not know it. The first thing I had to do was to admit I didn't just have a temper, but that I had an anger problem. Admitting we have a problem and asking for help is very difficult. Some think asking for help is a sign of weakness. I used to think this way. I no longer think this way anymore. I now know that asking for help is a sign of strength. Of course, I never thought of myself as a strong person. It was scary admitting I had an anger problem. What was this person (Bonnie) going to think of me? What was I going to have to do? Since she is a Christian counselor, was religion going to be "rammed down my throat"? If you have anger issues, just admit it. Find a counselor and get help. You may feel (like I did) that it isn't working. Don't believe it. It is working. It's like putting on weight. It doesn't happen overnight. It takes a long time to get you to the point of needing help and even longer to admit it. It will take a long time to get you back to where you should be. A happy person, a person at peace, a person that loves her/himself. And I don't mean in love with yourself. Think about it. We must love ourselves before we can love others. We live with ourselves twenty-four hours a day, seven days a week and 365 days a year. If we don't like (or love) ourselves, we cannot give that love to others.

God is with us and will always be with us. If we just talk to Him, He will always answer us. Sometimes it is yes, sometimes it is no and sometimes it is not right now. What we think we need isn't necessarily what we need. Only God knows what we truly need. Most of what we think we need is really what we want and don't need. Talking to God does not have to be flamboyant. Just talk to Him like you'd talk to a friend. He is your friend. He will be with you through the good times. He will also be with you and get you through the bad times and you will come out on the other side a changed and stronger person. I am a changed person. I am no longer an angry person. I am at peace and I am happy.

> *"I can do all things through Christ who strengthens me." (Philippians 4:13) NKJV.*

> *"Therefore, since we are surrounded by such a great cloud of witnesses, let us throw off everything that hinders and the sin that so easily entangles. And let us run with perseverance the race marked out for us, fixing our eyes on Jesus, the pioneer and perfector of faith," (Hebrews 12:1-2a) NIV.*

> *"And we know that all things work together for good to those who love God, to those who are the called according to His purpose" (Romans 8:28) NKJV*

REMINDERS FROM GOD

At the time of this writing, as I mentioned before, I moved back to the east coast. Just over 3 weeks after I moved, I was notified that my house had been broken into and ransacked. Unfortunately, it would be another 2 weeks before I could get back to see what had been done. From the day I was told about this, I could have sunk into a very angry state and gone into a rage. I had neither of these feelings. As a matter of fact, I did not realize I had not felt anger until after I had seen the condition of the house. Even then, I didn't feel anger. I started doing some thinking and realized God was reminding me every day since the notification that He is with me throughout all of this. Each day I get a scripture sent to me from WBCL by text message and a notification from The YouVersion Bible App. Here are a few I received throughout all of this.

11/7/2018

"I thank God for you." (2 Timothy 1:3a) NLV

11/12/2018

"The God of love and peace will be with you." (2 Corinthians 13:11) NLT

11/14/2018

"Each time he said, "My grace is all you need. My power works best in weakness." So now I am glad to boast about my weaknesses, so that the power of Christ can work through me." (2 Corinthians 12:9) NLT

11/14/2018

"....Remember, the Lord forgave you, so you must forgive others." (Colossians 3:13) NLT

11/19/2018

"Therefore, if anyone is in Christ, he is a new creation; the old has passed away, behold the new has come." (2 Corinthians 5:17) ESV

11/20/2018

"O Lord, I will honor and praise your name, for you are my God. You do such wonderful things!

You planned them long ago and now you have accomplished them." (Isaiah 25:1) NLT

11/23/2018 -This is the day I walked into my house.

"Yet what we suffer now is nothing compared to the glory He will reveal to us later." (Romans 8:18) NLT

11/25/2018

"The Lord is close to the brokenhearted; he rescues those whose spirits are crushed." (Psalm 34:18) NLT

11/27/2018

"Ask me and I will tell you remarkable secrets you do not know about things to come." (Jeremiah 33:3) NLT

As you are reading these verses, you might be wondering how these told me that He was with me. How could God let me go through this alone. I was not alone. I have learned over the years that HE is with me. God is the only true judge. The people that broke into my house (as will all of us) must stand before God on judgment day and answer for the things they (and we) had done during our lives. He will make the final judgment as to where we will all spend eternity. Yes, I am upset and disappointed that there are a lot of things that were stolen that can never be replaced. But it really does me no good to get full of anger and rage. That is what Satan wanted me to do. But God is around me and helping me through this. I was fully expecting that I would completely break down once I walked into my house. Yet I didn't. Yes, I was shocked as to what I was seeing, but I did not break down. We just started working on picking things up. When we were getting ready to leave, I remembered I had not looked at one of my daily scriptures. I looked at the one for that day and it is the one from **Romans 8:18 "Yet what we suffer now is nothing compared to the glory He will reveal to us later" (Romans 8:18) NLT.** This was so appropriate for that day. That day is probably one of the worst days of my life. But God was reminding me that *"it does not compare to the glory He will reveal to us later".*

ARE YOU A PRODIGAL SON OR DAUGHTER?

Christ never said we would be without trials. As a matter of fact, He said the complete opposite in that we would have trials.

In *James 1* He says,

> **Consider it pure joy, my brothers and sisters,[a] whenever you face trials of many kinds, because you know that the testing of your faith produces perseverance. Let perseverance finish its work so that you may be mature and complete, not lacking anything. (James 1:2-4) NIV**

During the healing process, there will be pain. To heal, you will most likely have to relive the pain of what people did to you. You will have to face the things that happened to you in the past or where you are at now. This was the hardest part for me. It was also the first time I connected emotionally with being molested and raped. I cried during my whole counselling session that day. When God knows you are ready for what He has been preparing you for, no devil in Hell can stop it.

Paul writes,

> **What shall we say about such wonderful things as these? If God is for us, who can ever be against us? Since he did not spare even his own Son but gave him up for us all, won't he also give us everything else? (Romans 8:31-32) NLT**

Only God knew when the right time was that I could emotionally deal with what had been done to me as a child. That time was three years after I moved to Indiana and within the first year of counselling. God's timing is not the same as our timing. We want it now, but God knows when it is best for us to receive it.

This morning in church, I was reminded again that we will have pain, and go through storms in our lives. We will come through the storms and will come out stronger. God does not cause the storms. Sometimes they are of our own doing and sometimes it is Satan. We had no control over it, but we are in the middle of it.

In the *Gospel of* **Luke 15:11-32**, Jesus tells the story of the Prodigal Son. I think that we are all like the prodigal son. I know I was. When I was growing up, we went to church every week. Then when I was out on my own, I walked away from church. Unlike the prodigal, I don't think mine was a conscious decision. It just happened. Once I was in counselling, Bonnie gave me a Bible and I started going back to church. We are all children of God. Like the father of the prodigal son, God was saddened when I (or you) walked away from Him but rejoiced when I came back to Him. He will rejoice when you come back to Him too.

Also in **Luke 15:3-8** is the Parable of the Lost Sheep. Jesus says,

> ***"I tell you that in the same way there will be more rejoicing in heaven over one sinner who repents than over ninety-nine righteous persons who do not need to repent" (Luke 15:7) NIV***

He is faithful. He loves us all the time no matter how we act. He doesn't like the sin we commit, but He does still love us unconditionally.

Do you think you have an anger problem? Maybe it's not anger. Maybe your problem might be depression, alcohol, drugs, pornography or even something else. Maybe you're in an abusive relationship. Maybe you're the abuser. God loves you no matter where you are. The first step is to admit you have a problem, no matter what it is. Anger does not have to become the rage and then danger. Maybe it already has and that is why you now realize you have a problem. Seek out counselling and seek out God. He will be (and already is) there for you if you just ask. He will lead you to the right place for help. What I am remembering is that I did not seek out God before my counselling. Remember, I had said I had walked away from Him. However, He led me to the right person, Bonnie, who then lead me through the healing and back to God. He knew I needed Bonnie.

WE ALL CAN CHANGE

I know I spoke of change previously, however; I need to come back to it. Today, at Church I was reminded again about change. We get excited about change until it starts to happen and then we fear it. Maybe even dislike it. It is said there are 365 times in the Bible where God tells someone do not fear or do not be afraid. I searched but could not find 365. I did find many and included anxious or worry which are both part of fear. Here is one of them. ***This is my command — be strong and courageous! Do not be afraid or discouraged. For the Lord your God is with you wherever you go (Joshua 1:9) NLT.*** I look back and see that with every move I made to a different state and/or a new job I was fearful and anxious. That is until I moved to Maine. From the time I turned in my notice at the bank I had not had any fear or anxiety at all. The time I was out of work was 45 days. I had never once felt fearful or anxious. I was completely at peace. No anger or discouragement. God was (and is) with me (and you) always.

I'm now attending The Rock Church. In today's Church service, the message was about building relationships. There were a couple quotes they used, and I will use here.

"Who you are is who you will attract," John Maxwell.

"Every relationship will only be as strong as the weakest person in it," Les Parrot.

Both quotes gave me ah ha moments. I was a broken person and I attracted broken people into my life. Some of these people caused me to be even more broken. Since I attracted broken people that brought me down, my relationships were not strong. Well, maybe they were strong, but in the wrong way. They were strong but in the weak sense because they were weak. But the weakness was a stronghold.

One of my favorite movies is A Christmas Carol. I especially enjoy the two older versions. One had Alastair Sim and the other had Reginald Owen. Both played Ebenezer Scrooge. I never really thought about it until now, but Ebenezer was a very angry man. If you've seen it, you will remember the evening of Christmas Eve, he was visited first by the ghost of his deceased partner, Jacob Marley. In the afterlife, Jacob was condemned to wander the earth in shackles and chains because of his selfish ways. Jacob came to warn Ebenezer to change his ways or else he would be condemned to the same afterlife.

ANGER RAGE DANGER

The ghost of Christmas past reminded Ebenezer what happened to him at boarding school. The parents of all the other kids had come to pick them up for the break. However, Ebenezer's parents never came, and he was left alone at school. I think, if this were to have happened to any of us, at some point we would resent our parents and become angry. The next ghost was the ghost of Christmas present. This one showed Ebenezer how he was acting and showed him that Bob Cratchet and his family were happy even through all the struggles they were having. Then finally, there was the ghost of Christmas yet to come. This ghost showed Ebenezer what would happen if he kept on the same course with his actions. If you think about it, like Jacob was warning Ebenezer, God is warning us to change our ways or suffer the consequences. As we know, Ebenezer did change. He became a happy person who was now willing to give to others. We need to change our ways or spend eternity separated from God.

As I think back on this movie, I can relate to both Ebenezer Scrooge and Jacob Marley. Most of my life, I was walking around in shackles because of my anger, depression, selfishness, control, and probably other things. These were all strongholds in my life and if I had not changed, I would have been condemned to eternity, separated from God, in shackles and in the darkness. I work at this every day with God's help. If I backslide in any area, I just ask Him to help me. To my friends, I may have seemed like I was a happy and outgoing person. This could not have been further from the truth. I am a very shy and introverted person.

Over the past few weeks at church, the messages have been about restoring ourselves spiritually. This week it was about fear and anxiety. If we allow these things to consume us, it is because we are not trusting God. All we need to do to get past this is to pray and ask God to take them from us and He will. Jesus says:

Ask and it will be given to you; seek and you will find; knock and the door will be opened to you. For everyone who asks receives; the one who seeks finds; and to the one who knocks, the door will be opened. (Matthew 7:7-8) NIV

So, I say to you: Ask and it will be given to you; seek and you will find; knock and the door will be opened to you. For everyone who asks receives; the one who seeks finds; and to the one who knocks, the door will be opened. (Luke 11:9-10) NIV

Yes, God is omnipotent and omnipresent. He knows everything and is everywhere. He knows what we are thinking and what is in our hearts. Since He wants a relationship with us, He wants us to ask Him for His help. He will always answer. Sometimes yes, sometimes no and sometimes not right now.

Recently, I went to see the 35th Anniversary showing of Karate Kid. Boy, did I see this movie with different eyes. When it originally came out, I was about 25 years old, which meant at that time I was an angry person. When I saw it for the first time, I don't recall really seeing that Daniel was being bullied. But that's exactly what was happening. This realization really took me back to my being bullied in elementary school and I started to cry. Remembering being chased, hit punched and called names. When Daniel wanted to learn karate, it was for all the wrong reasons. He wanted to use it for revenge and to fight. But the teaching he was given by Mr. Miyagi was something he could take as life lessons. As we all should. Not everything is what it seems. These lessons gave him confidence and thus was able to win the tournament without resorting to illegal moves. Yes, he may have been angry the way the other competitors were trying to cheat to win, but he kept his cool and came out on top. At the end, his nemesis congratulated him and told him he's all right. There is nothing wrong with confidence in ourselves. It's when we get cocky and prideful that our strengths will turn into weaknesses and will ultimately backfire on us and we end up losing. There are a lot of movies out there that are good quality movies, that teach life lessons.

Why is it that we think that getting angry or in a rage will always change things for the better? Being angry the right way most often will change things for the better. But how often do we get angry the right way. Often, we fly into a rage and expect people to do what we want. As a matter of fact, the only person we can change is ourselves. In life now a days most people are going to do what they want no matter the consequences. The rule book (the Bible), has been, thrown out the window so to speak. If something offends us, a physical fight can ensue, or someone takes the other person to court.

LOFTY GOALS AND PERFECTIONISM

I hadn't thought about it much until today. God triggered my memory of my having to be a perfectionist. I remembered that when I worked at the bank, we had to take online compliance courses. I had got to a point that I could not just pass. I had to get 100 percent on each one. I think all we needed to pass a course was a 75 percent. This meant that if I got one question wrong during the test, when I got to the end, I had to get out of the program and start over. A lot of the questions were recycled. So, this meant I knew the answers to some. If I had answered every question right and got to the last question and it was not one that I knew the answer to, then I would get out of the program and start it over. However, I had to have a perfect score. During the last couple of years I worked there, I realized I didn't have to be perfect. I just had to pass them. So, I began just working only to just pass the tests and not necessarily have a perfect score. It also meant that I didn't have to spend so much time on them since I no longer had to be perfect. This perfection was also a result stemming from my childhood. Not

LOFTY GOALS AND PERFECTIONISM

doing good enough to please my mother. My dad had always said if I gave my best effort to something, it was ok even if I didn't get a perfect score. I was never an honor roll student in school. But I did pass all my courses and graduated high school. I have no idea when this feeling of having to be perfect started. Perfectionism will do nothing but create frustration and then anger because we get frustrated about not being perfect. At the bank, we had new loan files that need to be serviced for different things. My job was to look at them for insurance compliance. These files were in copy paper boxes on a shelf. When I would get to work, I would have my goals set that I needed to get through three to four boxes. No matter how hard I tried, this was not possible. But I had to keep this goal every day. This was a self-imposed goal not one that was set by my supervisor. So, at the end of every day, I was never satisfied with the amount of work that I had accomplished. I was always focused on what I didn't accomplish. I would say, "I only got through two boxes not three". Oh, what I didn't mention was that part of my job was also to take phone calls or make phone calls. But I still was never satisfied with what I had accomplished. If I only had a couple pieces of paper that needed to be filed instead of a stack of papers, I didn't get anything done that day. After years of this, I finally got it together and began to look at what I had accomplished and not be focused on what I didn't accomplish. The issue I had was that I would always set goals for myself that were not attainable. What's worse is that it took way too long to figure it out. I would just always stay frustrated and mad at myself.

No one can or ever will be perfect. Perfection means that a mistake had never (and never will) been made. There is only one perfect person and that is Jesus Christ. That is why we must accept Jesus Christ as our Lord and Savior and when we ask God for forgiveness, our sins are covered by Christ's blood and all that God sees is a perfect person. This is also what grace is all about. We do not deserve either grace or forgiveness. All we deserve is eternal separation from God.

Throughout the whole Bible, it talks about imperfect people. God used imperfect people all for His purpose. Adam and Eve sinned. But if it were not for them, we would not be here. Moses did not speak well and he murdered an Egyptian. Jacob tricked his brother out of his birthright and blessing from his father. Saul (who became Paul) was a terrorist. He was out to persecute and kill Christians. God also calls people who are not qualified to do things He wants done. Were any of His disciples qualified to be disciples when Jesus called them to follow him? I don't think so. But they were all used for God's Glory. Here are six of Christ's disciples and their "qualifications". There was Simon who, was later named Peter and his brother Andrew, James, son of Zebedee, and his brother John. They were all fishermen. Matthew was a tax collector. Another Simon was a zealot.

The Merriam-Webster Dictionary defines **zealot** as:

"a zealous person; especially a fanatical partisan"

"a religious zealot"

"capitalized: a member of a fanatical sect arising in Judea during the first century A.D. and militantly opposing the Roman domination of Palestine"

ANGER AND RAGE RESURFACING

I mentioned earlier that I had moved back to Maine to help my sister, Patti, with the everyday things to do with our mom. I had been staying in the same house she and my brother-in-law occupy until I found a place to live. This is the same house that our mom and her late husband had owned. A few months after I got here there was an incident that triggered my anger and full-blown rage. I heard some very vile words being said by my brother-in-law to Patti. These words were so bad that I had to leave the house for a few hours. When I got back, I went to the basement, where I was staying, and everything was fine for a while. Then I heard things said to Patti about me. My name wasn't mentioned, but due to the situation, it was about me. I came "unglued." Remember I had dealt with my anger many years ago and I thought it was gone completely. I went upstairs and confronted my brother-in-law. It turned into my having a "melt down." I started yelling at him and said that for whatever reason he didn't "have the guts to confront me" about issues he had with me. He tried to back pedal and say that what he had said had nothing to do with my sister or me. I'm not going to repeat here what he said to Patti that was so vile. But he tried to say it had to do with what he was watching on television which was wrestling. This was so far from the truth. What was said, had absolutely nothing to do with wrestling. What he had mentioned was about the ring on her finger and the ring she wears on a chain around her neck. The things he said to Patti about me had to do with moving in. When I mentioned this, he said he was talking about the cats. I said, "the cats didn't just move in." I kept going on and on and was so angry I was shaking. I was so scared about how I was feeling and reacting. Patti came out of the bedroom to try to calm me down. Unfortunately, I would have no part of calming down. When I was finally done, I looked at them and said, "you both need to sober up!" He said, "so here we go!" I said, "I didn't say you need to sober up, I said "you both need to sober up!" Patti hugged me and said thank you. I don't know why. I went back downstairs and started to cry. I was still shaking.

Whenever I had got this way in the past, I did not recall myself shaking. I prayed to God and asked for forgiveness. I asked Him to tell me if the way I acted in my anger was righteous or sinful. I never did hear words from God, but my crying stopped in a very short amount of time. It took me a couple days to realize that God may have answered me in that moment that maybe I had not sinned, by my crying stopping quickly. I had not felt like this in years. I don't remember ever shaking when I was in a rage. Which as I'm writing this, I realize I was in a rage and not just anger. It took me about a week to get over this. I had to get right with God and right in my soul about this. I was (and still am) ready to interact with both Patti and her husband. What is very sad is that since that fateful day, I have not seen either one of them at all at the house. They hide in one of the bedrooms and I'm assuming wait until I get there at night and then they come out. I normally don't get to the house until 6:00-6:30 at night and I don't hear anything for at least an hour or two. My sister does work an overnight shift, so I don't see her anyway. However, she has three days off and I don't even see her on those days. This makes me very sad. She is my only sibling and neither one of us had kids. I had thought we would have a relationship when I moved here. The only time I do see her Is once a week when we both see mom on the same day. And this is for only about 20 minutes once a week. That's all the time I get to have with her.

THERE IS HOPE YOU ARE A WORK IN PROGRESS

My plan throughout this book is to show you that even though we are an imperfect people, and we all have struggles, we will survive.

I used to attend a church called The Rock. It had two campuses, one in Bangor, ME and the other in Old Town, ME. I attended a service at each campus on Sundays. Both campuses teach the same message each week. I first heard the message given by Pastor Kirk Winters in Bangor and then went to Old Town where I heard the same message again by Pastor Buddy Eckman. What was interesting is that I always got a little something different out of each message. This was so helpful with my continued walk and journey with Christ and God.

The following has been taken from the sermon series we just had, and I have permission to use it.

This past Easter, we ended a three-week sermon series on Hope. I'm here to tell you that whatever you are dealing with, you will get through it. Three weeks ago, was the Sunday before Palm Sunday. This was the day we started this series on Hope. It is titled

"Hope Has a Name". We were reminded about both suffering and hope and how they go together. Would you believe that there is a purpose for our suffering? Until now, I certainly wouldn't have thought so. Suffering can be good for us. But it can also cause us to lose hope if we don't look at it in the right way. We should be seeking God all the time, in both the good and bad times. But if we seek God in our suffering, we can have hope that He will help us through it. The Bible does not say that we will never have trials. As a matter of fact, it says just the opposite. It says we will have trials. James writes:

> ***Consider it pure joy, my brothers and sisters, [a] whenever you face trials of many kinds, because you know that the testing of your faith produces perseverance. Let perseverance finish its work so that you may be mature and complete, not lacking anything (James 1:2-4) NIV***

There are three different perspectives to consider about suffering. They are the past, present and future. We tend to look at all three of these in the wrong way. But I'm going to show you the wrong and right perspectives of each.

The wrong perspective of the past when we are suffering, is to look at the past and say, "I wish I were back there," no matter how bad it was. For whatever reason, we only see the good part of the past.

When we hope for the past, we get discouraged in the present. Yes, I suffered during my childhood and in my early years as an adult, but the past is what has made me into the person that I am today. I can't change the past, but I can learn by it and go forward. I am now a much stronger and more positive person. The right perspective of the past should be that I will remember all of what God has done. If it weren't for my suffering, I would not be doing what I'm doing today.

Paul says,

> **May the God of hope fill you with all joy and peace as you trust in him, so that you may overflow with hope by the power of the Holy Spirit. (Romans 15:13) NIV**

What's in between suffering and what we hope for is a waiting period. We don't like to wait. We are by nature impatient. But the suffering and the waiting makes us stronger if we are willing to change our views of both. Periodically I do look back at the past. But not to wish I were back there. I look at the past to see where I am today and to see how much God has done for me and in me.

I had a "melt down" a few months ago. But I got over it. In the past, I would still be holding a grudge for months towards Patti and my brother-in-law.

This is not the case now. I got over it quickly. Yes, I'd like to have the relationship back with them. It may never happen and I'm ok with that. I am not angry at them, I still love them, and know it's their loss to not have a relationship with me. This is a waiting period. Yes, I hope that they will come around and want to have a relationship with me. But, in this case, I am not suffering. It's not worth it to get myself all worked up at something that may or may not happen. I'm not sure if they are both still holding a grudge or if one is holding the grudge and is controlling the other to not have contact with me. All I can do is give it to God and have Him work on each of them. Remember, God does do miraculous things if we just let Him. Let go and let God.

    The wrong perspective of the present is that we sometimes think about what is happening to us and say, "this is a big waste of my time." This is what I remember about how I felt during the beginning stages of my counselling. I remember thinking, "it's not working and I'm wasting my time". That was my wrong thinking. Of course, had I not been in the mental state I was in, the right thinking would have been "this is an opportunity." But as I mentioned before, at that time I was not walking with God so I couldn't have had a right perspective of anything, let alone of the present. God is always moving in us even when we are in the waiting periods of our life. Don't give up. It is not a waste of time. Remember, (an analogy) we didn't put the weight on overnight, it will not come off overnight.

In the book of **Galatians 6**, Paul talks about reaping what we sow. He writes:

> *Whoever sows to please their flesh, from the flesh will reap destruction; whoever sows to please the Spirit, from the Spirit will reap eternal life. Let us not become weary in doing good, for at the proper time we will reap a harvest if we do not give up. Therefore, as we have opportunity, let us do good to all people, especially to those who belong to the family of believers. (Galations 6:8-10) NIV*

Waiting is not a waste of time. It's an opportunity for us and God is moving in us and through us. We cannot see the big picture, but God does. Only God knows why I still didn't have the relationship back with Patti and my brother-in-law. But I have learned to wait on Him. He knows the right time to bring that back around if He chooses to. I saw something today that said something to the effect of if God showed us the big picture, we wouldn't even take the first step. This is so true. If God had told me a long time ago that I would write a book, I probably wouldn't have started it because I'm not qualified to be a writer.

The wrong perspective of the future is that we get so focused on the finish line and we forget what's happening now. We ask, when will this ever end? Life is a journey. In running terms, life is a marathon not a sprint. I remember when I started running. I was thinking when will this end when I was only running 60 seconds!! Two years later I was running my first half marathon and loving it. Back when I was running just 60 seconds, I never fathomed that I would be running a half marathon. We don't notice the waiting during the good times. We only notice the waiting during the hard times.

Yea, though I walk through the valley... (Psalm 23:4a) KJV

This valley is a waiting period. During our suffering, we forget that there is always a purpose for it. We are so focused on the negative, which ends up getting us distraught. We try to "fix" it ourselves and get discouraged. The future will fix itself. All we should be focused on, is the present. We don't even know if we will be here tomorrow, so why worry about it. Tomorrow is not a guarantee.

The right perspective of the future is to ask, "Who will I be when this is over?" I decided I will get through this.

***The steps of a good man are ordered by the Lord...
(Psalm 37:23a) KJV***

God is focused on the journey. God also cultivates us during the waiting. Like a garden, during the waiting, you cultivate it so that in the future you will have a harvest. Do you worry about a garden? Probably not. You just go about cultivating the garden. To find hope in the waiting, we need to change our perspective. We can't go back. We can't change the past, so don't worry about it. Since we don't know if we will even be here tomorrow, don't worry about it. The only thing there is, is today, the present. It's called the present because it is a gift from God.

I first went over the bad news about our suffering. Now for the good news of Hope. Hope is not wishing. Hope is theological and comes from our belief in God. The further we get away from Christ, the less hope we have. However, the closer we get to Christ, the more hope we have.

There are three kinds of Hope. They are:

Wishful Hope - This is what we use most of the time. "I hope I win the lottery". I hope our team wins. In a sports metaphor, it's the Hail Mary pass in a football game. In both cases, it's just wishing. Not really Hope. No guarantee at all.

Expectant Hope - There is no guarantee with this either, but it is a stronger hope than wishful hope. This would be most like planting a garden. We expect to have a crop or flowers. When a woman is pregnant. She is expecting but there is still not a 100 percent guarantee that it will go well.

Certain Hope - This is a guarantee. It's the anchor in our lives and only found with God. Just like an anchor on a boat, which keeps it from drifting, God is our anchor. If we put our trust in God, we have certain hope. God is Hope.

For the most part, we are just drifting through life. Unbeknownst to me, this is what I was doing most of my life. I didn't have the "anchor" in my life, Christ. If I had the "anchor" in my life, things would not have been as they were. But that's ok. We just wish our lives away. Hope is not wishing. Hope is theological. It comes from our belief in God. Certain Hope creates a stability and makes us stronger. Hope is the anchor that can keep us from drifting.

> **We have this hope as an anchor for the soul, firm and secure... (Hebrews 6:19a) NIV**

When we are drifting in life, we are not safe. God has people in our lives that will say just the right thing at just the right time to give us hope. Real hope is based on God's words not our wishes. The further away a person gets from God, the less hope we have. The closer a person gets to God, the more hope we have.

> *Can papyrus grow tall where there is no marsh? Can reeds thrive without water? While still growing and uncut, they wither more quickly than grass. Such is the destiny of all who forget God; so perishes the hope of the godless. (Job 8:11-13) NIV*

When we get away from God, we tend to look for hope in all the wrong places. We will wither away. With my anger, depression, and negative attitude, I was withering away and didn't even know it.

The Ten Commandments show us just how broken we are in that we can't keep them. These are the basics, and we can't even keep ten rules. We've all broken just about all of them. In life, there are so many more to live by. We are a broken people. We are sinful by nature, but the hope is that God still loves us even through our brokenness. If we seek Him, we will find Him.

There are a lot of causes for hopelessness. Here are the ten most common causes:

Feelings of abandonment - Disappointments in life

Life seems out of control - Things will never change. I can't fix this.

Don't see a purpose for our pain – Why am I suffering this way.

Grieving a loss - Loss of a loved one, job, health.

We don't have what we need - If I just had more opportunities.

We've done something wrong - Feelings of guilt or regret

Deeply wounded by someone - Abused, betrayed

Pulled in a wrong direction - Constantly being tempted or giving into it.

Hounded by fear - Anxiety

When it looks like defeat - Looks like it will not go well for you.

I'll admit, I can say I have felt all of these at one time or another. In some cases, I brought it on myself. In other cases, it was caused by someone else. Lastly, in the rare case it was both.

But you know what? There are ten reasons for hope. There is an "antidote". It is the Lord's Prayer and is found in **Matthew 6:9-13.** I'll use the King James Version which is the version we are most familiar with. Along with each verse (or part of a verse) will be the meaning.

Our Father who art in heaven, - He will never abandon us.

Hallowed be thy name - God's power is greater than any problem.

Thy kingdom come, - God fits everything into his plan. *(Romans 8:28)*

Thy will be done on earth as it is in heaven - God has a greater purpose for my life.

Give us this day our daily bread. - God has promised to daily, meet all my needs.

And forgive us our debts, - Jesus died to pay for all I've done wrong

As we forgive our debtors - God will settle the score someday

And lead us not into temptation - God promised to help me

But deliver us from evil: - Jesus in me is greater than any other power

For thine is the kingdom, and the power and the glory forever. Amen   THIS IS NOT THE END OF THE STORY

    I am still a work in progress. My anger - rage for the most part is gone. My depression is gone. My low self-esteem is gone. Satan is the author of hopelessness, guilt, anxiety, and other negative issues in us. Satan likes to stay in the dark and keep us in the dark. So, if we bring these things out into the light, Satan cannot thrive. There may be a day when my anger will rear its ugly head again like it did a few months ago. When (and if) this happens, I have the hope and faith that God has my back and will not let me be tempted to sin in my anger. But if I do sin in my anger, I will ask God for forgiveness. Remember, there is righteous anger and sinful anger. Human anger is most often the sinful kind. I may have a day when I feel hopeless. I will then have to consciously get my head back in the right place and remember that there is Hope and it's in Jesus. Right now, my living situation is not good. But I am not discouraged, and I don't feel hopeless. I know that at the right time, which is God's timing, I will find a place of my own. Until then, I don't need to worry about it.

Let go of control. Surrender your heart to God. Repent of your sins. Ask for forgiveness. Once you do that, He will help you. You do not have to be "fixed" before you can be a child of God. I wasn't. He wants all of us. He loves all of us no matter what we have done. It will take time to feel the peace and joy that God wants us to have, and that's ok. It took 13 years for me. It might take you less (or more) time. Just be patient.

Hope Has a Name. That Name is Jesus Christ.

You can get through anything with His help. Just ask. He loves you.

Remember

And we know that all things work together for good to those who love God, to those who are the called according to His purpose. (Romans 8:28) NKJV

AND

I can do all things through Christ who strengthens me. (Philippians 4:13) NKJV

At the time of publication, my sister, Patti lost her husband suddenly in August 2019 and then 6 months later, in February 2020, we lost our mother due to end stages of Alzheimer's. I have also moved back to Indiana. And in 2021 my counselor Bonnie passed from COVID.

ENDNOTES

Introduction

Definition of Anger – *Meriam Webster Dictionary* On-Line

Definition of Rage – *Meriam Webster Dictionary* On-Line

Definition of Danger – *Meriam Webster Dictionary* On-Line

Chapter 3 – Admitting I Had a Problem

Definition of Bible Belt – *Meriam Webster Dictionary* On-Line

Chapter 4 – The Healing Process

Romans 8:28 (NKJV)

Chapter 5 – What Is Love?

1 Corinthians 13 – *Good News for Modern Man* (1966 Edition)

Chapter 9 – Visionaries ABF and Telling of My Anger

Matthew 5:3-9 (NIV)

Chapter 10 – Forgiveness, Grace and Mercy

Mark 11:25-26 (NASB)

Luke 23:34 (NIV)

Definition of Convict – *Meriam Webster Dictionary* On-Line

Definition of Condemn – *Meriam Webster Dictionary* On-Line

Definition of Grace – *Meriam Webster Dictionary* On-Line

Definition of Forgiveness – *Meriam Webster Dictionary* On-Line

Definition of Mercy – *Meriam Webster Dictionary* On-Line

Song Title: Tell Your Heart To Beat Again - (CMG Song# 102885)
Writers: Randy Phillips
Matthew West
Bernie Herms

Label Copy: Copyright © 2014 Awakening Media Group (ASCAP) (adm. at

CapitolCMGPublishing.com) All rights reserved. Used by permission.

Tell Your Heart to Beat Again
Words and Music by Bernie Herms, Matthew West and Randy Phillips

Copyright © 2011, 2012, 2014 SONGS OF UNIVERSAL, INC., G650 MUSIC, PURE NOTE MUSIC, GET UR SEEK ON. AWAKENING MEDIA GROUP, SONGS OF SOUTHSIDE INDEPENDENT MUSIC PUBLISHING and SONGS FOR DELANEY

All Rights for G650 MUSIC and PURE NOTE MUSIC Administered by SONGS OF UNIVERSAL, INC.

All Rights for GET UR SEEK ON Administered by DOWNTOWN DLJ SONGS

All Rights for AWAKENING MEDIA GROUP Administered by CAPITOL CMGPUBLISHING.COM

ENDNOTES

All Rights for SONGS FOR DELANEY Administered by SONGS OF SOUTHSIDE INDEPENDENT

MUSIC PUBLISHING

All Rights Reserved Used by Permission

Reprinted by Permission of Hal Leonard LLC

TELL YOUR HEART TO BEAT AGAIN

Words and Music by BERNIE HERMS, RANDY PHILLIPS and MATTHEW WEST

© 2014 SONGS OF SOUTHSIDE INDEPENDENT MUSIC PUBLISHING, SONGS FOR DELANEY, EXTERNAL COMBUSTION MUSIC, BANAHAMA TUNES, AWAKENING MEDIA GROUP, ALTAS MUSIC GROUP and BERNIE HERMS

All Rights on behalf of Itself and SONGS FOR DELANEY Administered by SONGS OF SOUTHSIDE INDEPENDENT MUSIC PUBLISHING

All Rights on behalf of AWAKENING MEDIA GROUP Administered CapitolCMGPublishing.com

All Rights Reserved

Used by Permission of ALFRED MUSIC

Chapter 11 – Running and Endurance

Philippians 4:13 (NKJV)

Matthew 7:13-14 (NLV)

Hebrews 12:1 (NIV)

Chapter 12 – My Baptism

Romans 6:3-4 (NLT)

Song Title: Cornerstone - (CMG Song# 58921)

Writers: Edward Mote
Reuben Morgan
Jonas Myrin
Eric Liljero

Copyright © 2012 Hillsong Music Publishing (APRA) (adm. in the US and Canada at

CapitolCMGPublishing.com) All rights reserved. Used by permission

Chapter 14 – The Big Picture and God's Plan

Isaiah 61:3 (NLT)

Jeremiah 29:11 (NIV)

Ezekiel 36:26-27 (NIV)

Isaiah 41:10 (NIV)

Romans 8:28 (NKJV)

Chapter 16 – God's Love, Anger and Punishment

Genesis 16-19 (NIV)

Genesis 6:6-8 (NIV)

Matthew 21:12-13

Chapter 17 - Give it to God

Ephesians 4:26-27 (NIV)

Philippians 4:13 (NKJV)

Hebrews 12:1-2a

Romans 8:28 (NKJV)

Chapter 18 – Reminders from God

2 Timothy 1:3a

2 Corinthians 12:9 (NLT)

ENDNOTES

2 Corinthians 12:11 (NLT)
Colossians 3:13
2 Corinthians 5:17
Isaiah 25:1 (NLT)
Psalm 34:18 (NLT)
Jeremiah 33:3 (NLT)
Romans 8:18 (TLB)

Chapter 19 – Are you a Prodigal Son or Daughter?
James 1:2-4 (NIV)
Romans 8:31-32 (NLT)
Luke 15:11-32
Luke 15:7 (NIV)

Chapter 20 – We all Can Change
Matthew 7:7-8 (NIV)
Luke 11:9-10 (NIV)
Joshua 1:9 (NLT)

Chapter 21 – Lofty Goals and Perfectionism
Definition of Zealot *Meriam Webster Dictionary* On-Line

Chapter 23 – There is Hope – You are a Work in Progress
James 1:2-4 (NIV)
Romans 15:13 (NIV)
Galatians 6:8-10 (NIV)
Psalm 23:4a (KJV)
Psalm 37:23a (KJV)
Hebrews 6:19a (NIV)

ANGER RAGE DANGER

Job 8:11-13 (NIV)
Matthew 6:9-13 (KJV)
Romans 8:28 (NKJV)
Philippians 4:13 (NKJV)